Too *Amazing* for Coincidence

Heavenly Interventions

Too Amazing for Coincidence

True Stories of God's Mysterious Ways

Heavenly Interventions

EDITORS OF GUIDEPOSTS

Too Amazing for Coincidence: Heavenly Interventions
Published by Guideposts
100 Reserve Road, Suite E200
Danbury, CT 06810
Guideposts.org

Copyright © 2024 by Guideposts. All rights reserved.

This book, or parts thereof, may not be reproduced, stored in a retrieval system, or transmitted in any form or by any means, electronic, mechanical, photocopying, recording, or otherwise, without the written permission of the publisher.

Cover and interior design by Judy Ross Graphic Design
Cover photo ©YOTUYA iStock/Getty Images
Typeset by Aptara, Inc.

ISBN 978-1-961126-57-2 (hardcover)
ISBN 978-1-961442-32-0 (softcover)
ISBN 978-1-961126-58-9 (epub)

Printed and bound in the United States of America

*We declare God's wisdom,
a mystery that has been hidden
and that God destined for
our glory before time began.*

—1 Corinthians 2:7 (NIV)

Contents

A Foot and a Half from Heaven – *Louis Lotz* 1
Message in a Dream – *Courtney Ellis* 5
Let Go – *Leanne Jackson*. 10
The Candy Apple Urge – *Betty A. Rodgers-Kulich* 15
Stuck in a Storm – *Rebecca Hastings*. 20
The Banquet Hall Miracle – *Andrea Jo Rodgers* 25
I've Got to Thank Stella! – *Roberta Messner* 29
Three Shiny Nails – *Carol Round* 34
Affirmations from God – *Heather Jepsen*. 39
A Helping Hand – *Linda S. Clare* 45
From Uptown Girl to God's Girl – *Kimberly Davidson* 49
God's Gift Card Provision – *Tina Wanamaker* 55
A Late-Night Knock – *Darci Werner* 60
The Accident That Wasn't – *Sandra Kirby Quandt* 65
Marrying the Monogram – *Virginia Ruth* 69
A Prayer and a Policeman – *Carol Gimbel*. 74
I Can Only Imagine – *Kathleen Stauffer*. 80
Long Shot – *Bethany Sheldon, as told to Marci Seither*. 87
The Flow Blue "Accident" – *Roberta Messner* 92
Near Abduction in Broad Daylight – *Liz Gwyn* 96
Stranded – *Denise Margaret Ackerman* 102
The Blue House – *Linda H. Summerford* 107
The Right Call – *Alice H. Murray* 110
Stopped by an Angel – *Toby Williams, as told to
   Ellen Fannon*. 115
God's Perfectly Timed Text – *Juliette Alvey* 118

Miraculous Distractions – *John Smith, as told to Mindy Baker* 123

One Small Mistake, One Amazing Gift – *Michelle Stiffler* 130

Remarkable Peace – *Renee Mitchell* 135

God Sees – *Elsa Kok Colopy* 141

When One Open Door Leads to Another – *Laurie Davies* . . . 144

All That I Needed – *Penny L. Hunt* 149

God Towed My Heart to Safety – *Linda S. Clare* 151

Six More Months – *Wendy Klopfenstein* 155

The Cruise That Never Ends – *Becky Alexander* 161

Blind Faith – *Leah Vidal* 167

"You're Alive" – *Angela J. Kaufman* 173

Instant Comfort – *Rhoda Blecker* 177

For Such a Time as This – *Kenneth Avon White* 182

Pointing Me in the Right Direction – *Diane Stark* 188

The Wind – *Lowell Bartel* 192

A Sister-in-Christ from God – *Nyla Kay Wilkerson* 196

A Voice from the Flames – *Ellen Akemi Crosby* 200

The Power of Secret Giving – *Diane Buller* 206

The Eleventh Hour – *A. J. Larry* 211

Storm Shelter – *Nancy Shelton, as told to Marci Seither* 215

God's Divine Delay – *Nicole N. Brown* 219

Thankful for Stomach Pain – *Melissa Henderson* 222

Golden Chariots Don't Run on Fumes – *Sarah Greek* 226

A Prayer Quickly Answered – *Barbara Jean Deaton* 229

The Only Night We Needed Help – *Jesse Neve* 233

If Only Mother Were Here – *Roberta Messner* 236

Acknowledgments 242

Editor's Note 243

A Foot and a Half from Heaven

Louis Lotz

*His lightnings light up the world;
the earth sees and trembles.*

—Psalm 97:4 (NRSVUE)

We bought the place—my wife, Mary, and I—not so much for the house, but for the property—a sprawling acreage complete with an apple orchard, rows of raspberries, a forest of sycamores and sugar maples, and a kelly-green meadow bordered by a little stream. It was perfect. A house you can remodel, but the land is what it is, and we loved the land.

The house remodeling took months, but finally the big stuff was finished—knocking down walls, expanding rooms, renovating the kitchen and bathrooms. Now the only job left was staining the woodwork. Initially, the guy we'd hired to do the work said that he was busy on another job and he wouldn't be able to get to us until the next week. But then, a pleasant surprise—the staining guy finished his other job way ahead of schedule, and he showed up at our place bright and early the next morning and began unloading his truck. Mary and I had moved into the house and were living there, the renovation notwithstanding, but now Jack, our builder, said, "You might want to sleep somewhere else tonight. The fumes from the stain and the shellac will give you a monster headache."

I said we'd be OK. "We'll just shut the bedroom door; the fumes won't bother us."

But Jack was insistent: "Please, you shouldn't stay here in the house, it's just not safe. Really, those fumes will make you sick."

I was reluctant to pay for a hotel room, even if I could find a vacancy on such short notice. But Jack said that he owned a rental property that happened to be vacant just now, and we were welcome to it, no charge. Problem solved. So my wife and I grabbed our toothbrushes and a change of clothes and away we went. The sky was the color of a bad bruise, and you could tell that a storm was on the way. It was first day of summer 2002.

The phone rang early the next morning, around 5 a.m. I remember thinking as I reached for the phone, *whatever this is, it is not good.* It was Jennifer, a co-worker. "Are you OK?" she gasped. "Where are you? Is Mary with you? Thank God you're alive!" She'd heard via one of our neighbors that our house was on fire. We'd left one of our cars in the driveway, and Jennifer was afraid that we'd returned to the house.

By the time we arrived, the house had burned to the ground. It was smoldering rubble, with sinuous ghosts of smoke writhing upwards. Sooty firefighters drenched in sweat waded through the rubble with handheld extinguishers, chasing the final few flames. Our new home, all our possessions, gone.

It turned out that the fire had been started by a stray bolt of lightning from the storm the previous night. The fire chief showed us where the lightning had hit—a metal gas pipe that fed into the house. The pipe had been twisted and shredded in the explosion, creating a giant blowtorch effect, sending gas-fed flames roaring through the house. The wet shellac and the fumes fueled the fire even more. "We got here as soon as we could," the fire chief said, "but she was already engulfed in flames. We saw your car and assumed you were in the house. I sent in a couple of my boys, trying to find you, but the flames were too intense, and the roof was about to go, so they had to get out. Thank God you weren't in there."

I kept staring at the mangled gas pipe, which entered the house by the master bedroom, about eighteen inches from where my head would have been lying on the pillow. You lay your head on the pillow at night, and it never occurs to you that you might be a foot and a half from heaven.

I kept staring at the mangled gas pipe, which entered the house by the master bedroom, about eighteen inches from where my head would have been lying on the pillow.

The most important things in life are your faith and your family, and both of them were OK. They didn't get so much as singed. Nobody got hurt. Losing all your possessions is hard, of course. Granted, most stuff can be replaced—furniture, clothing, appliances. But some items are beyond replacement. Family photos. The stuffed rabbit our daughter slept with when she was child. Mary's wedding dress. The two-handed sippy cup our son drank from when he was a toddler. Books. Homemade quilts. There's no replacing things like that.

The insurance company has you list all the items you lost in the fire, and in the ensuing weeks that's what we did, Mary and I—we tried to remember and list how many pair of shoes we'd lost, how many shirts, how many belts, books, tools, chairs, tables, and on and on. You have no idea how much stuff you've accumulated until you have to list it all. But as I went through the list, my mind kept drifting back to that mangled gas pipe where the lightning hit, about eighteen inches from where my head would have been, and I kept hearing the fire chief's gravelly voice saying, "Thank God you weren't in there."

I began doing just that—thanking God. I thanked God that the guy who stained the woodwork showed up ahead of schedule at my home, forcing my wife and me to spend that night elsewhere. I thanked God that Jack the builder was insistent that Mary and I not spend the night in the house, and that he owned a rental property that just happened to be vacant. I thanked God that my head happened to be lying somewhere else when that 300-million-volt shaft of lightning struck the gas line, engulfing the house in flames. Some people might call that coincidence, but I know different. It is no coincidence when God provides. It is no coincidence when God protects. As the saying goes, "Coincidence is God's way of remaining anonymous."

Message in a Dream

Courtney Ellis

Some things have to be believed to be seen.
—Madeleine L'Engle

When my contractions began, my birth plan evaporated.

"Get the keys!" I gasped, waking my husband, Daryl. He untangled himself from the sheets and gathered his wits.

"OK," he said groggily. "OK, OK, OK."

I'd planned my maternity leave carefully—with only six weeks of time available to me, I didn't want to waste a moment. Yet here I was, ten days overdue, watching precious leave slip away. I'd tried the home remedies—bumpy car rides and spicy food and raspberry leaf tea—but there was still no sign of impending labor. At my most recent doctor's visit, when the receptionist greeted me with a chirpy, "You're *still* pregnant? Your due date was over a *week* ago!" I wanted to scream. I'm an arrive-early person; if a task is due on Friday, I'll get it to you by Thursday at the absolute latest. But this first baby was coming on its own slowpoke schedule. Plus the last few weeks of pregnancy can be incredibly physically uncomfortable. I felt—and looked—as if I'd swallowed a watermelon.

Daryl and I had been living on the edge of our seats since I had crossed into my ninth month of pregnancy. Our hospital bags were packed. We kept the car filled with gas. But on this particular night, I'd thrown my hands up in resignation. Clearly the baby would never come. Might as well get some sleep! Together we'd finally fallen into our first deep sleep in days. After weeks of telling each other *it could be any minute,* we'd completely worn ourselves out.

But here we were, scrambling for our shoes at 3 a.m. At long, long last, it was time.

"OK," Daryl said once more, rubbing his eyes and staring at me in bewilderment.

"Let's GO!" I said through gritted teeth, breathing hard through another contraction.

"We are planning to labor at home for a bit, right?" He gathered his bearings. "I can call the hospital and let them know your labor has started."

"Nope!" I said. "Change of plans. My contractions are already five minutes apart. They *started* at five minutes apart." The force of the labor pains that catapulted me from sleep was a shock. I was a distance runner—discomfort was a familiar friend. My capacity for enduring physical misery was one reason we'd planned for a natural birth. I could handle a good bit of pain; I had lots of strategies for taking my mind to happier places. But the severity of these contractions was a new level. I tried to approach it with interest and not fear.

"This baby is going to come quickly, I think," I said. Daryl pulled on his jeans, threw our bags into the car, and helped me to my seat.

Farmland sped by outside our windows, frosty in the chill of a September night. The almost-full moon shone on stacks of hay, casting long shadows across newly harvested fields. I tried to take in the peace of the landscape, willing myself to relax. *Tension is the enemy of a gentle birth,* my doula taught me. *The more you can soften, the better.*

Help me, Jesus, I prayed aloud. *Help me, help me, help me.*

Daryl pulled our car into the hospital lot at 4 a.m. and we walked through the triage doors, trailed by our doula, who'd arrived a few minutes prior. Anna smelled of lavender and spoke in low tones, placing a firm hand on the small of my back.

"You've got this," she said, her confidence buoying me.

Help me, Jesus, I prayed.

Once we arrived in the labor and delivery room, a nurse checked my progress.

"You have a long way to go," she said. "You're only four centimeters dilated." She called my midwife, Dr. Kate, and told her not to come until her hospital rounds began in several hours. "This baby won't be here soon," she said.

I labored for a short while in the tub, breathing the prayer that had gotten me this far. Then something shifted. Where there had once been intense but manageable pain, a wave of such fury washed over me that my body writhed, muscles spasming out of my control. I screamed.

"Courtney," the nurse told me, quickly appearing from the hallway, "get onto the bed." When it came time to push, mothers were required to get out of the water.

"*No,*" I said.

"Courtney," said Daryl, "the nurse needs you on the bed."

"*No!*" I said. "I can't!"

"Courtney," said our doula, "it's time to get on the bed."

"*NO!*" I yelled in desperation. "None of you understand! I can't *move! It hurts too much!*" I thrashed in the tub as the three people trying so desperately to help me looked at one another, exasperated. I couldn't articulate it then, but part of my stubbornness came from knowing that not one of them had ever birthed a baby. They didn't know my pain from the inside, so I didn't trust them to help me through it.

HELP ME, JESUS! I shouted internally.

Suddenly, a new voice from the doorway.

"Courtney, get on the bed." It was Dr. Kate. In our months of prenatal meetings, Dr. Kate had shared her own birth stories with me. Three children. All over ten pounds. No epidural. Together we'd laughed over my ultrasounds and the baby's kicks and hiccups. As we built a friendship, together we mourned the bumps in the road of her vocational journey: she felt called to be a pastor, but her church wouldn't allow it.

"Well, you're certainly ministering to *me,*" I told her. I'd never received such tender, professional care. I trusted Dr. Kate with all my heart.

At 5 a.m., Dr. Kate found me in agony, still in the tub, and terrified to push. The one person I trusted to walk me through the most physically intense moments in my life arrived at exactly the moment I needed her. She waited out my next contraction and then grabbed my hand.

"This is the moment," she said. "Let's get you on the bed to push."

An hour later, our firstborn son was nestled in my arms.

As the nurses tidied the room and Daryl and I acquainted ourselves with our baby's impossibly tiny fingers and surprising shock of dark hair, we remembered the conversation we'd overheard. Dr. Kate wasn't supposed to come in until eight when her medical rounds began, yet she'd appeared in my room at five.

The one person I trusted to walk me through the most physically intense moments in my life arrived at exactly the moment I needed her.

"Maybe she was called in for something else," Daryl mused, sliding his hand down my arm to interlock his fingers with mine.

"Probably," I agreed.

When Dr. Kate came back to check on me, he raised the question.

"How did you know to come early?" Daryl asked her. "We heard the nurse tell you that Courtney wouldn't need you for hours yet."

"I went back to sleep," she said, "but God sent a dream that Courtney needed me right away, so I got up and started driving."

Our eyes met over my bundled son, sleepy from his journey.

"Thank you," I whispered.

"Jesus heard those prayers," she said, and then chuckled. "And so did the rest of the hospital." We grinned. Dr. Kate laid a hand over mine for a few seconds, nodded at Daryl, and returned to her rounds.

What a story. What a God.

Let Go

Leanne Jackson

I can do all things through him who strengthens me.
—Philippians 4:13 (ESV)

I was exhausted after our move to Indiana. I grieved the family and longtime friends I'd left behind, and I was still unpacking boxes. Again. This had been our second interstate move in six months, and I had used up all my enthusiasm the first time. Every day I prayed for strength.

One blessing of this move was my decision to homeschool my daughters; we enjoyed studying together. And when I'd signed up Katie, age eleven, and Emily, age seven, for homeschool drama and swimming classes at the Y, I met homeschool moms who were slowly becoming friends.

Then a major January snowstorm hit, and we were stuck inside for days. After finishing our schoolwork, we snuggled under quilts to read books. We made a game of propping open cupboard doors to keep the pipes from freezing. I called my father on his birthday to boast of my new lifetime record—minus 22 degrees. But you couldn't shovel the icy mess, and you certainly couldn't play in it.

The first day the Y opened, we headed out. The girls climbed into our minivan and buckled their seat belts. I edged slowly through our slippery neighborhood. The thick layer of ice didn't concern me; I had learned to drive in upstate New York and driven safely through many snowy winters.

However, our first summer in central Indiana had been a shock, with all that humidity. Wasn't the Midwest supposed to be dry? It didn't occur to me that humid air would also surround Indiana on subzero days. Nor did I know that high humidity plus bitter cold is a recipe for "black ice." Invisible ice.

I drove cautiously, surprised that so many cars had ventured out. On my right I noticed a puzzling sign, "Bridge freezes before roadway." Yes, we were approaching a bridge. But it was way up ahead, spanning the White River. I didn't realize that this road was actually a long, curved ramp—the first section of that bridge.

Without warning, the minivan began to fishtail. The chatter behind me abruptly stopped. I grimly concentrated on the road. I tapped the brakes, as I'd been taught, but our speed never slowed. Steering was my only hope. I wrestled with the steering wheel, jerking it left to avoid the approaching guardrail, then right to miss an oncoming car. We wobbled our way forward, my frantic efforts alternating faster and faster. The two-lane bridge sped swiftly toward us. We were going to hit something, and soon!

I cried out, "Lord, HELP!" *Did I speak those words aloud?* A firm male voice commanded, "Let go!"

Nonsense! I argued inwardly with the voice. *I'm gripping this wheel, this tiny bit of control. Letting go would send us over the edge, for sure!*

The voice sounded louder, more insistent. "Let GO!!"

I argued, this time with myself. *I did ask for help. How can I refuse? Time is running out* . . . With huge misgivings and a knot in my stomach, I let go of the wheel.

Immediately, I regretted it. I tried to capture the steering wheel, but it spun mightily around. *What have I done?*

The car whirled forcefully, trying to fling me aside. My seatbelt gripped my chest and hips like a giant vise. My dizzy brain registered: *we're facing the wrong way!* We hurtled between the oncoming cars toward the other side of the bridge. Beyond the guardrail I spied an angry, steel-gray river, farther below than I'd thought. Preparing to plummet into it, I must have closed my eyes.

One loud *CRUNCH*. We lurched, stopped. Silence.

Dazed, I opened my eyes. *We're not in the river! We're not tangled with another car!* Vehicles were passing us, easing around the minivan. We were upright, still on the road. We— *my daughters!*

I whipped my head around. Both girls were still in their seats, eyes wide, silent. Alive! Katie's lip bled a little. Emily rubbed her head. I reached my hand back; they grasped it with both of theirs.

A stranger stopped his pickup truck and ran to my window. "Is everyone OK?"

I nodded mutely. He walked around our minivan, inspecting. He reported that one side was caved in where we'd bounced off the guardrail, but the other side, where we all sat, appeared undamaged.

This was before cell phones, so I wondered aloud how to call a tow truck. He pointed out, "Your car's still running! I bet you could drive it. Tow trucks might be too busy today."

Slowly, shakily, I drove us home.

That night my muscles felt stiff and sore, but my mind was twirling, turning over all that had happened. We had been gaining momentum, heading toward that bridge, out of control. Why had we not plunged into the river?

God's angel must have seen the single safe way to release our momentum: my car had to spin during the one break in traffic across that narrow bridge.

My own strength was not enough. I had to let go.

God's Mysterious Ways: The Voice

When God works in our lives, sometimes it's huge—a miracle that everyone can stop and marvel at. But sometimes it's the still, small voice that we read about in Scripture (1 Kings 19:12), the one that speaks directly to our soul and our circumstances.

In this volume, we have several examples of people saved from a dangerous situation, or guided toward a blessed outcome, by a voice that seems to come out of nowhere: God speaking to them, guiding them in a time of need.

Have you ever sensed that inner guidance? Would you like to be more open to it? Here are some steps you can take:

- **Pray.** If you have a routine prayer time, take a moment during that time to intentionally ask God to guide you—to let you hear His voice when there's something He wants you to do (or not do!). If you don't have a routine prayer time, set yourself a goal of praying this question every day or two.

- **Seek.** Be open to God's voice, even when it's just a small nudge. If you come to a point in your day when you have a decision to make, pause intentionally and listen to see if God has a direction for you.

- **Act.** If you hear that voice, act on it!

- **Reflect.** After you've acted, think about what happened as a result. What might have been different if you hadn't been listening?

The Candy Apple Urge

Betty A. Rodgers-Kulich

Many are the plans in the mind of a man, but it is the purpose of the LORD that will stand.
—PROVERBS 19:21 (ESV)

On August 25, 1965, I was a thirteen-year-old only child on a two-family boating excursion of the Great Lakes. Bored with being confined to my parents' cabin cruiser, I was looking forward to spending the day without parents at our next stop—Boblo Island, home to a Coney Island-style amusement park. Our parents were looking forward to a great dinner, entertainment, and fellowship while I, along with the two teenaged sons of the other married couple on the trip, rode rides, ate carnival foods, and generally enjoyed ourselves.

After mooring, our parents purchased the entrance tickets and gave us money for food and souvenirs. I joined up with David, fourteen, and Ronnie, seventeen, who was "volun-told" to look after us. Our parents had been friends since we were little, so though the boys were like older brothers, sibling rivalry wasn't an issue, and it didn't feel like being watched by a sitter. It was going to be a great evening.

Our plan was to hit every ride in the park. It was a Wednesday, and the lines were shorter without weekend crowds, allowing us to walk up and get right on. As the sun began to fade, the park came alive with festive, multicolored lights, adorning the white picket fences surrounding the rides in rainbow colors. We indulged in every traditional carnival treat we could find as we made our way around the park, hoping our stomachs would not rebel. The night was turning into the best part of the vacation yet.

Nearing the end of the evening and rides, we headed to the popular ride called the "Tumble Bug" because it looked like a giant caterpillar. Each car was separate from the others, connected to a central hub by a long, metal arm that propelled each car up and down the ten-foot-high looped track.

We laughed at the fact that for once we had a wait line to ride. Counting the seats and the people in line ahead of us, I figured we should be able to get on in the next group.

While waiting with anticipation at this park's favorite ride, wafting on the evening breeze came the smell of fresh candied apples. Suddenly, I was filled with urgency: I *needed* a candy apple. I spied the vendor under a group of trees and reached into my pocket to discover that my funds were running low. I'd planned to get a souvenir, but if I bought the candy apple, I wouldn't have enough left for anything else. But in that moment, the urge welled up and won—the decision was made. I'd get a vacation souvenir another day.

My mind made up, I turned back to wait for our group to board. It seemed like forever as the aroma continued to tantalize me. The urge grew. The ride attendant was chatting up two teen girls—totally oblivious to the extra time he was allowing the current riding group to squeal and scream with joy. I became convinced I had time to run over, purchase that enticing candy apple, and stash it inside my cloth shoulder bag before our turn to ride.

Ronnie and David protested my plan, but I convinced them by pointing out that the ride attendant's flirtatious conversation would buy me time. I would be over and back before the ride ended. My pleading eyes overcame their remaining protests, so I took off running, letting my nose lead the way before they changed their minds.

Suddenly we heard a loud crack and snap, like sound effects out of an action movie.

As I was stuffing my wrapped treasure into my bag, I heard the boys yelling for me to hurry. Apparently, the ride attendant had finished his flirtation and the current riders, eager to get their land legs back, quickly disembarked. I ran as fast as I could, but before I got to our place in line, the boys had to tell the group of kids behind us to go on ahead and take our seats. The ride was now filled. We would need to wait for the next ride cycle.

The boys glared at me. I apologized profusely.

"Why couldn't it wait?" one of them demanded. "There wasn't a good reason for you to go right then."

I shrugged. "I don't know." I *didn't* have a good reason. I'd just been overwhelmed by that sudden urge.

The boys gave me the cold shoulder, turning to watch the Tumble Bug. It was flying around the track, arching up and down, bringing screams of delight and pleasure.

Suddenly we heard a loud crack and snap, like sound effects out of an action movie. The next thing we knew, a car had broken free from one of the arms and flipped freestyle like a bucking rodeo bull, throwing the car's occupants free from the car, into the air, and down onto a picket fence. The heavier car tumbled and landed between the fence and the ride. Ecstatic screams suddenly changed to piercing cries of pain. Shocked, traumatized witnesses gasped in fear, weeping and making inarticulate sounds. The ride stopped without any more cars falling, but the state of those kids was unknown.

Park first-aid rescuers came quickly, but the difficulty would be transport. The mainland hospital could only be reached by ferry or private boats. A somber announcement from the public address system blared out, directing everyone to leave because the park would be shutting down immediately. The boys and I walked toward our parental meetup location in stunned silence. My knees were weak, and I felt sick to my stomach.

As we walked, Ronnie stopped suddenly and said, "Do you guys get what just happened? The car that flipped would have been our car. The kids thrown out were the ones we let go ahead because you were late getting back in line. It would have been *us!*"

Ronnie's words hit me with the enormity of what could have been. I wiped the start of a tear away and my arm brushed against my bag with the candy apple bulge. Had that sudden craving for a candy apple come for a reason?

The reality of life and death hit us that evening. Later we would hear that one of the kids died from injuries suffered in that freak accident. Why had we been spared? At bedtime, my usual half-hearted prayers were a mixture of grateful tears for our lives and safety and tears of sorrow for a lost life. For reasons unknown, God's intervention had saved us—had saved me. Yielding to that urge for a candy apple had made all the difference in our fate. That night I became aware of God's intervening hand in my life and my destiny.

As my faith walk has matured, I pay attention to those "random" thoughts from God. I have learned to trust and obey His life-changing and lifesaving directions! My destiny has been forever changed.

Stuck in a Storm

Rebecca Hastings

I am going to send an angel before you to protect you on the way and bring you to the place I have prepared.
—Exodus 23:20 (CSB)

The weather forecast was clear: a winter storm was headed our way. The school I taught at dismissed early, and I was grateful for the head start on the storm. The roads seemed clear when I set out, wet with just a hint of the precipitation that was to come later—or so I thought. Once I began heading north, I knew I was wrong. I quickly ran into a curtain of heavy snow that had already obscured the road.

I followed the tire tracks of cars before me, trusting they knew where the yellow line hid beneath the snow. I took my time as the snowflakes fell and my wipers cleared my view. My fifteen-minute ride home had already taken me twice that, and I still had one more turn to make.

The street sign was covered by snow, but I needed no reminder of the name. Great Hill Road was not the most ideal place to drive in the middle of a snowstorm, but I had no choice. My house was at the top of the winding road that led to the bluff.

I made the turn knowing I needed speed to make it up the hill. I took advantage of the flattest area at the beginning of the road and wound my way up the first incline. As the road became steeper, I felt my tires losing their grip.

I tried desperately to correct my sliding car, but I slipped back to the sharp curve at the tree line before my car came to a stop. Looking in my rearview mirror I saw a narrow swath of trees and then nothing but snow falling into the valley beyond. In any other situation, it would have been beautiful.

Easing my foot on the accelerator only brought me closer to the trees behind me. With my foot pushing hard on the brake pedal, I sat in my car. The only sound around me was the ice and snow pelting my windshield.

The beauty of living on a road like Great Hill Road was how peaceful it is. You can easily go for hours without a single car passing by. Not a comforting thought when you have a hill in front of you, a valley behind you, and icy snow threatening to send you over the edge. Taking out my cell phone, I tried to think of who to call. My mother was closer than my husband. I dialed the number and prayed.

She answered quickly, but she couldn't get out of her driveway to help me. Even though my husband was working at the hospital more than a half-hour away, I called him for help. There was nothing he could do. He checked with the police and fire department. They could add me to the list of stranded motorists, but it was a long list. The storm came faster than anyone expected. No one could help me.

As we talked, an old white pickup truck drove up the hill past my car and stopped. I had never seen this truck, and Great Hill Road was not the place for new drivers to explore in a snow and ice storm. A man got out of his truck and moved closer. Without saying anything he began looking under the front end of my car.

I sat there quietly for a moment, not sure what to do. I couldn't take my foot off the brake, and I had never seen this man before. He stood up and approached my window. I took in his appearance. He wasn't young, but he wasn't old either. His worn pants and weathered face matched his beat-up truck.

"You stuck?"

I nodded quickly. "Yes."

"I've got a chain. I'll pull you up the hill." And without waiting for an answer, he walked back to his truck and grabbed a heavy metal chain.

I couldn't understand how this would work. How was he going to make it up the hill with the ice and snow? Never mind doing it while pulling another car. He finished chaining my car to his truck and came over to my window.

"Now, just keep your foot on the brake a bit to keep tension on the chain. Understand?"

"Wait. So you're going to pull me and my whole car up the hill?" My words came out slowly with sign-language-like hand gestures to make sure we both understood what was going to happen.

"Yes." No hesitation; no sign of concern. Just a patient, matter-of-fact response.

I nodded, wide-eyed and confused but without daring to open my mouth. I watched the stranger walk confidently to his truck. As he started the pickup I felt a tug on my car and I focused on the only thing that made sense to me: keeping my foot on the brake. As the truck pulled my car around the first corner of the hill, I felt my car sliding to the left and watched him adjust his path.

My hands gripped the steering wheel as we climbed higher, my car slithering side to side and narrowly missing trees along the way. We made it past the stone bridge and up the last section of the hill to where the road levels before I saw his brake lights shine through the snow.

Watching him calmly unhitch the chain from my car and put it back in his truck, I sat in disbelief and gratitude. Who was this stranger in the white pickup who had just pulled me up Great Hill Road?

I sat in disbelief and gratitude. Who was this stranger in the white pickup who had just pulled me up Great Hill Road?

He headed toward my car again and stopped a few feet shy of my open driver's window. I didn't dare take my foot off the brake for fear of sliding back down the incline he had just rescued me from. The stranger spoke before I could. "You take care."

"Wait. Thank you so much. My name is Becky. I live right around the corner in the little cottage by the field." I began taking my glove off to hold my hand out for him to shake and introduce himself, but he only waved behind him as he moved toward the white pickup. I watched his taillights ahead of me, leading the way until I turned into my driveway.

As I entered my warm house, I called my husband to let him know I was home safely; that the man had pulled the car up the whole hill. When he asked which neighbor helped me, I told him I'd never seen the man before.

After that cold, snowy day I was always on the lookout for that old white truck, but somehow I knew it wasn't from around here.

The Banquet Hall Miracle

Andrea Jo Rodgers

*He performs wonders that cannot be fathomed,
miracles that cannot be counted.*

—Job 5:9 (NIV)

I've been a volunteer emergency medical technician on my local first aid and rescue squad since high school, answering over 9,300 rescue calls over the past thirty-five years. On the night these events happened, our team had been called out to the Whispering Winds Banquet Hall, responding to an emergency call for a man whose heart had stopped beating. The impressive multistory brick restaurant dazzled many with its five-star meals and high-end services. We rushed along a shaded cobblestone path and up a flight of concrete steps to the entrance.

A worried-looking hostess with shoulder-length, curly brown hair held the door open for us, pointing to a large room toward the right. "He's in there."

As I entered the ballroom, I could see it was set up for a wedding, with white lace and gorgeous spring flowers adorning the space. Rows of padded folding chairs faced a large table and podium at the front of the room. A middle-aged man with an ashen-white face lay flat on his back in the center of the aisle. A man with short gray hair who appeared to be in his early fifties knelt next to our patient, performing vigorous chest compressions. A younger man with shaggy blond hair squatted on the patient's other side. One of our town's police officers, Jack Endicott, provided rescue breaths by squeezing a bag-valve-mask (BVM) hooked up to 100 percent oxygen.

A second police officer, Ethan Bonilla, looked up from operating the defibrillator. "Our patient is a sixty-two-year-old male named Hank Edwards. He's here attending a wedding with his wife. Without warning, he passed out while sitting in his chair and fell into the aisle." He paused and nodded toward the man doing chest compressions. "Dr. Jones is a cardiologist. He was sitting directly across from Hank and immediately began CPR. The florist's husband is an EMT, and he is assisting."

Dr. Jones glanced upward while continuing to perform chest compressions. "We defibrillated once so far without regaining a pulse."

The young man with the blonde hair stood up to make room for the squad members. "We were able to start working on him within seconds. I'm just glad I happened to come with my wife today."

One of my team members, Kerry Branson, began setting up the suction equipment just in case we needed it, carefully attaching the suction tubing to the unit and running a bit of sterile water through it. Another, Sadie Martinez, pulled an oral airway from our first-aid bag and sized it by measuring from the tip of Hank's ear to the corner of his mouth. She deftly inserted it to help maintain his airway. I noticed he didn't gag at all. *He's completely unresponsive.*

"I'm going to analyze. Everybody clear," Officer Bonilla said, waving his arm over Hanks's body to ensure no one inadvertently touched the patient.

At that moment, Hank's eyes fluttered open. "What happened? Did I pass out or something?"

"Prepare to shock," the semiautomatic defibrillator's tinny, recorded voice announced. The machine began creating a whirring noise as it drew energy from the battery. Officer Bonilla pressed the shock button, causing powerful joules of energy to course through Hank's lifeless body. I said a quick silent prayer it would restart his heart.

Officer Endicott slid his fingers into the groove at the side of Hank's neck. "I've got a strong carotid pulse. Hold compressions." My heart filled with hope. His heart beat again, though he remained unconscious and wasn't breathing on his own.

A third team member, Helen McGuire, placed a blood pressure cuff around Hank's left upper arm. "His blood pressure is 104/60 and his heart rate is 96 and strong." *A good sign.*

A few minutes later, Hank's color seemed less ashen as a pink hue infused his cheeks. In the tug-of-war between heaven and earth, earth seemed to be gaining an advantage.

"He's beginning to breathe on his own now. I'll get a non-rebreather ready," Helen said, preparing a mask and a second oxygen tank. A non-rebreather mask provides high-flow oxygen to patients who can breathe on their own.

At that moment, Hank's eyes fluttered open, and he yanked out the oral airway. "What happened? Did I pass out or something?"

His wife, who had been standing nearby, brushed tears from her cheek and jumped to her feet. "Honey, we're here for a wedding."

Hank attempted to sit up. "Really? Who's getting married?"

With those lucid questions, I realized Hank stood an excellent chance of not suffering any brain damage from his time without a heartbeat. *A true blessing.*

More people began arriving for the wedding. Hushed whispers spread rapidly among the concerned guests. We lifted Hank onto our stretcher and rolled him to the ambulance, loading him in for transport to the hospital. Hank shook his head and whistled softly. "I can't believe I passed out at a wedding. I feel fine now."

I adjusted the strap near his left cheek. "You're doing much better," I replied. Even as I spoke the words, I couldn't help but think I was staring into the face of a living miracle.

Thanks to immediate chest compressions from a God-sent cardiologist and the florist's EMT husband, Hank received lifesaving care within seconds of his cardiac arrest. If he had collapsed at home just a few hours earlier, it could have been a very different outcome. He wouldn't have been within mere feet of health-care professionals and a defibrillator. I marveled at how God placed the right people in the right place at the right time to care for Hank. Just a coincidence? I don't think so. Immediate access to lifesaving CPR followed by defibrillation contributed to saving Hank's life.

At the hospital, he underwent an emergency cardiac catheterization and angioplasty that very day and went on to make a full recovery. *A true banquet-hall miracle!*

I've Got to Thank Stella!

Roberta Messner

Give thanks in all circumstances; for this is God's will for you in Christ Jesus.
—1 Thessalonians 5:18 (NIV)

I'd picked up an order of chicken and was driving home when a thought came unbidden. Not a thought. An instruction. An urgent instruction.

Thank Stella!

Where did *that* come from? There'd been nothing to remind me of the freezing February night my father passed away. No emerald-green vans on the road like the one Dad had driven before he was diagnosed with cancer. No one wearing scrubs. No smell of coffee or the crackling sound of cheese crackers being unwrapped. Just the sudden memory of a nurse named Stella who had made our last moments with him bearable.

Dad's cancer had spread to his brain, lungs, and bone, but he'd been hanging on for weeks. The call came from the care facility that his breathing had changed, indicating that his condition was worsening quickly. We'd better come now. As the nurse in the family, I'd overseen Dad's harrowing struggle, the twelve-plus years of tests, treatments, and meds. Dad was worn out. I was worn out. My sister was worn out.

As Rebekkah and I entered Dad's room, Stella pulled us aside. "You made it! Your dad's been asking." The three of us circled his bed. My sister and I each squeezed a hand and watched his erratic breathing. Small puffs of air followed by no breathing at all. Cheyne-Stokes, they call it, a pattern familiar to nurses when patients near the end of their earthly journey.

Dad opened his eyes. We said our I-love-yous one more time.

"It won't be long," Stella whispered. "You two stay here and I'll be back."

Minutes later, a table and two carts rolled down the hall. Blankets and pillows were piled high on the table; the carts held a microwave, coffee pot, carafe of orange juice, packages of cheese crackers, bags of chips, and a foil-wrapped something . . . a cozy inn on wheels. Stella and two other staff set it up in the semiprivate room across from Dad. I'd seen it all in three decades of nursing. But never this.

"I want the two of you to get some rest," Stella soothed. "Push this button to start the coffee. Help yourself to the juice and snacks." She told us she'd baked the oatmeal raisin cookies before her shift, "just the thing if you nuke them a few seconds." She attached a call button to our fluffed pillows for whenever we needed anything.

Rebekkah and I managed a nap. At three a.m., I awoke to the sound of Dad's breathing. I tiptoed to his bedside for what would be our last words to each other. "You wouldn't believe what your nurse did," I said. "We have a home away from home right here with you." My father's eyes held mine one final time. Between ragged breaths, he managed three words

I'd heard since I was a little thing. Our private language of the heart.

"One in ten?"

There was a whole world in Dad's question. The hard life he'd endured as an orphan during the Depression and the people who'd helped him. His job on the railroad where he "got" to go work, never missing a day to provide for us. His battle with alcohol that led to a brand-new life of saying thank you by serving others.

I'd been slow to warm to the idea that gratitude mattered. Was the key to joy in any circumstance. One day I'd whined: "You help all these people, Dad. They don't even notice, much less appreciate it."

In the numb sorrow of Dad's passing,
I'd neglected to say thank you to
Stella for her kindness.

"You remember when Jesus healed those lepers?" he wanted to know. "There were ten of them. Only one said thank you. There's nothing worse than leprosy, honey. And that was *Jesus* they failed to thank. Always be that one in ten."

In the numb sorrow of Dad's passing, I'd neglected to say thank you to Stella for her kindness.

Now, twenty-one years later, I felt Dad pressing me into action with every fiber of my being. *You've got to thank Stella!* But so much time had passed. She was surely retired. If she was even still living, how would I ever find her?

Overcome with emotion, I pulled to the side of the road. My phone rang; it was a nurse who'd once inspected care facilities. "I just came from the Hospice House," she said. "Stella's there. Didn't she take care of your dad?"

Stella? She'd been to see Stella?

"It's bad," my friend continued. "Cheyne-Stokes respirations. Doubt she makes it through the night."

Stella was too ill for more visitors, so I called the Hospice House. I was just in time to tell her nurses about the treasure in their care. For them to pass along my gratitude for her special brand of comfort. The circle of caregiving would be complete . . . Stella and her dear ones surrounded by the kind hospitality Stella herself had offered.

The One who holds our times in His hands had brought His angel of mercy to mind. With not a moment to spare.

GOD'S MYSTERIOUS WAYS:
THE URGE

Sometimes God's direction doesn't take the form of a voice, but an impulse or urge that seems to come out of nowhere. Maybe you weren't thinking about calling that person, or going out to that particular store, or saying what you just said, but suddenly, there you are—in the right place, at the right time, doing just what needs to be done.

Maybe you'll find an opportunity to do God's work, to help a person who needed it in that moment. Or maybe it's you who needs help—to be saved from physical harm, to be brought back to safer paths.

Keep your spirit open to experiencing God's divine impulses. You might be surprised at how often He sends them your way.

- **Pray.** When you're in your prayer time, be sure to ask God how you can be of service to others. Ask Him to guide you to the place you need to be, when you need to be there.

- **Seek.** Do you have an impulse to do something unexpected? Of course, sometimes they really do come from our own minds, not from God. But if you feel the call, take a moment to sit with it. Turn it over in your heart, and ask yourself—and God—if this is really a calling.

- **Act.** If the urge persists, even if you try to ignore it— follow it and see where it leads.

- **Reflect.** Did you find an opportunity to do good when you followed that urge?

Three Shiny Nails

Carol Round

*In order to realize the worth of the anchor
we need to feel the stress of the storm.*
—Corrie ten Boom

Five hours after signing a contract to sell my house, tornado sirens started blaring. I grabbed my nine-month-old puppy, Harley, and huddled in my walk-in closet. My heart was racing as I listened to the howling wind. Debris hit my house, and I prayed for God's protection.

My cell phone simultaneously rang and pinged with text messages. My friends and family members, who heard the weather warning of an approaching tornado in my community, were checking on me.

I answered a call from my oldest son. "Mom, are you OK?"

"I'm in the closet with Harley. I'll be OK. Keep praying for us," I replied. After hanging up, I didn't answer any more messages or calls because my phone battery was at 25 percent and I wanted to save power in case I couldn't charge it later.

Sirens continued to blast as I clutched Harley to my chest. He kept wiggling, sensing my apprehension. The winds picked up, buffeting my house with what I assumed were flying objects caught up in the tornadic rage. My prayers continued for safety, not only for myself but for everyone else in the path of the tornado.

Just as suddenly as it had hit, the winds died down, leaving an eerie quiet behind. Should I leave the shelter of my closet? What would I find outside the confines of my safe haven? What destruction was I facing?

While I was grateful to be unharmed and alive with my new puppy, I was concerned about the damage to my house. Yes, things can be replaced, but the house I was purchasing in another town was under a thirty-day contingency contract. Major repairs could mean a delay in the closing; even worse, my prospective homebuyers could back out.

When I finally emerged to inspect the damage, I was relieved to find that it wasn't as bad as it could have been. The bedroom where I'd been taking shelter was undamaged. There was a hole in my kitchen ceiling the size of a truck tire, which I later realized had been bored by a flying leg from a neighbor's trampoline. Sand from a bag meant to hold the trampoline in place and insulation from the ceiling littered the downstairs, but the other damage was fairly minor.

Family members and friends showed up to check on me, including my friend Mike. They began placing tarps on my roof and removing debris blocking my garage door. Still in a daze, I hurried to my home office to locate my insurance information. My hands were shaking. I couldn't concentrate on the folder lying open on my desk.

Seeing my struggle, another friend, Lindsey, took the folder from my hands. "Let me look for the phone number," she said, patting me on the back.

I stood away from my desk to let her take my place in my office chair. When I did, I glanced at the wall where Mike was standing. He was holding Harley, who in all the excitement was struggling to get down.

As I reached to take my dog from his hands, I noticed three nails protruding from the wall. Driven straight into the sheet rock, they stuck out approximately an inch, and were spread out over an area about the size of a 5×7-inch picture frame.

Puzzled, I said, "Where did those nails come from? They weren't there before."

My youngest son, Clint, had just stepped into the room when I voiced my question. He replied, "Didn't you have pictures hanging there?"

"No," I said. "Remember when I decluttered my house before putting it on the market? I had a tall bookcase there before I moved it to another room. I never had anything hanging on that wall."

Frowning, my son replied, "Maybe you just forgot, Mom."

"No, I didn't," I said, reaching over to remove one of the shiny nails from the drywall.

"Look at this," I said. "These nails are new. They've never been used."

"What?" Mike and Clint blurted at the same time.

"Look," I said, holding up the nail for their inspection. "If it had been in the wall for a while, drywall dust would be clinging to the nail. This nail is clean—new."

Sticking the nail back in the wall, I pulled out another one. Clean. Poking the second nail back into the wall, I grabbed the third one. Clean. Puzzled, I looked at the others in the room.

36

"There must be an explanation. How would three clean nails show up on my office wall? The door was closed, and I don't keep any nails in my office."

"Are you sure, Mom?"

"Why would I keep brand-new nails in my office?"

All my tools, nails, screws, and other handywoman stuff were stored in the garage on the opposite end of the house. Glancing around, I saw there was no other damage in the room. No broken window. How did those three nails end up in my wall? A wall where nothing else had been, except a tall bookcase.

"There must be an explanation. How would three clean nails show up on my office wall? The door was closed, and I don't keep any nails in my office."

Then Lindsey pointed out something I hadn't noticed. "Do you notice the pattern of the nails?" She smiled at me.

Stepping away from the wall, I turned to face it again. I shivered as the realization hit me. There were three nails, but not just any nails. The nails—two at the top and one at the bottom lined up in a familiar pattern—an inverted pyramid. It was a reminder of two outstretched hands on the cross and the third at the foot. It was Christ on the cross.

"Wow!" The three-letter word seemed inadequate. No one spoke. Maybe it was the overwhelming presence of God's spirit in the a room only eleven feet wide.

Pulling me into a hug, my son said, "God was watching over you, wasn't He, Mom?"

As tears filled my eyes, I replied, "Yes, He certainly was."

Over the next several weeks, my house was filled with insurance adjustors, companies giving repair quotes, construction workers, and friends who helped with more of the cleanup aftermath. As each person entered my home, I excitedly led them to the wall where the three nails remained until I pulled them free to allow a repairman to fill the tiny holes and touch up the paint.

The couple who bought my house followed through with the contract and I was able to move on. Even so, I've saved those three shiny nails, placing them inside an empty prescription vial. I keep them in a safe place as a reminder of God's amazing grace. Too amazing for coincidence? You bet!

Affirmations from God

Heather Jepsen

Before our eyes the Lord sent signs and wonders . . .
—Deuteronomy 6:22 (NIV)

When I was in my twenties, God called me to be a pastor. While my life in ministry has had its ups and downs, over the years it often seemed like there have been a lot more downs than ups. Since the coronavirus pandemic, things have been especially hard. Like many churches, we had to deal with the sudden shift to online worship and deaths within the congregation. When the virus had passed, nothing really went back to normal. We are back to worship in the sanctuary together, but numbers are down, and folks are struggling to find the spirit.

Within my own life, the spirit felt absent as well. What economists called "the great resignation"—the time post-pandemic when many people were reevaluating their lives and leaving jobs they no longer enjoyed—hit churches hard. Many of my pastor friends quit the ministry. Some moved into chaplaincy instead of church work, but many others simply walked away. I too had times when I considered quitting, but I couldn't imagine another career I would enjoy.

One recent fall, things got really bad. There was a fight in the church, which happens sometimes, and I was bearing the brunt of people's anger and dissatisfaction. Many meetings featured raised voices, accusations of mismanagement, and threats to my job. I have been at this church for ten years, so I knew that some conflict was par for the course, but still, it cut deeply.

The conflict in my church, my own feeling of burnout, and everyone else quitting their jobs all seemed to add up. Soon I found myself in a negative spiral. At best I thought I should just walk away from ministry. At worst, I thought I had wasted my whole life.

Does my ministry make any difference? Have I thrown away the past twenty years? I was deep in despair and shame, and I turned to God in prayer. "God, help me to know what You want me to do. I've only ever tried to follow Your call. Is it time to leave?" I prayed.

I am nothing if not committed, so even though I was struggling deeply in my heart, I just kept plugging away at my job. And in the week after that desperate prayer, God met me, showing me in unmistakable ways just how much I was needed.

The first sign I had from God was during a meeting with a parishioner. Maggie came into my office on Tuesday morning to discuss a homeless ministry the church was considering. Once the business was done, Maggie and I just started talking. Like me, Maggie is fascinated by the power and presence of God in the world. We started wondering about answered prayer. "What happens when we pray? How does God hear us? How does God answer us? How does prayer affect healing outcomes?" Before we knew it, we had talked for two hours!

My conversation with Maggie was a reminder of how much I love talking to people about God. Sharing stories of faith is what lights my heart on fire. My time with Maggie felt like a divine nudge. God was saying, *Remember how much you love this? Don't quit now.*

Later that day I received a frantic phone call from Carol, the daughter of one of my parishioners. Her ninety-two-year-old father, James, was in the hospital. He was suffering from suspected internal bleeding and needed a scope, but they would have to put him under anesthesia to do the procedure. James had been told that at his age, he might not wake up again, and he had become terribly afraid. Carol wondered if maybe I had a few hours to spend to drive up to the hospital and see him.

God was with me; my afternoon schedule was open. James is one of my special longtime church friends, and so I made a few phone calls and hit the road. When I got to the hospital

My time with Maggie felt like a divine nudge. God was saying, Remember how much you love this? Don't quit now.

I patiently waited while James worked with the nursing staff. Masks were required in the hospital hallways, so my face was covered up. James clearly wasn't sure who I was.

When the nursing staff left, I sat in the chair to talk to James. As I took my mask down, Carol said, "Dad, Pastor

Heather is here to see you." James burst into tears. He was so moved that I would make the hour-long drive to see him in the hospital on such short notice. I was moved by his obvious thankfulness for my presence. Together we reminisced for a while, talking about happenings at the church, kids and family, and finally his upcoming procedure. James confessed that even though he had considered death before, the suddenness and immediacy of it was discomforting. I assured him that God was with him no matter what happened. We held hands and cried and prayed. When nursing staff returned, I knew it was time for me to leave. But in the visit the message from God was clear: *Heather, you do make a difference.*

Later in the week, I was busy leading worship at the local memory care home. My church comes monthly to lead a weekday worship service with the residents there. The service features scripture reading and prayer, but mostly it is singing. The old hymns are a great way to bring back memories for those who have lost some of their sense of presence and place.

At the end of the service after I give the benediction, I always go around the room shaking hands and offering a personal blessing to each individual. As I was making my way around the room, one attendee held my hand very tight. "Thank you for coming," I said. "God bless you."

"Who are you?" she asked.

"I'm Pastor Heather."

"Pastor Heather?" Her eyes filled with wonder. "It is an honor to meet you."

I smiled. "It's an honor to meet you too, ma'am." There was something in the way she looked at me—like she thought I was the Pope or something. *I hear You, God.* I thought. *I'm getting the message that I matter.*

When I got back to the office that afternoon, there was some mail on my desk. It looked like a Christmas card, but I didn't recognize the name on the return address. It had clearly gotten lost in the mail, because the envelope was stamped "undeliverable," and yet here it sat on my desk.

> *I hear You, God. I'm getting the message that I matter.*

I opened the card and began to read it. My eyes filled with tears. The card was from a woman in my community that I had never met. She had read an article I had written for the local newspaper titled "The Perfect Christmas." In the article I described how the first Christmas was far from perfect and encouraged readers to let go of their own longing for perfection around Christmas. This woman said that she had never had a good Christmas and always felt like such a failure. My message in the newspaper this year had inspired her to let go of her attempts to make the holiday something it wasn't. Without that baggage she had felt free, and it was the best Christmas celebration she'd ever had. "I can't thank you enough for your message of hope," she wrote.

I came downstairs to share the card with my church secretary, and she said the woman had walked it in to the office. Even though the post office returned her letter, even though she had never been to my church, even though she didn't know who I was, she made an extra effort to bring her note of thanks to me. She had no way of knowing that I had spent the week contemplating quitting, and yet her card was the icing on the cake for renewing my spirit. "OK, God," I said. "I hear You. I'll stay."

Life is a challenge for all of us, and everyone at some point begins to wonder if they matter at all. My week of affirmations from God was such a blessing. Through the voices of friends and strangers, I heard God clearly affirm my call to ministry and the work I do in the church.

Signs and messages from God can be anywhere. Sometimes all we need to do is just be on the lookout.

A Helping Hand

Linda S. Clare

Your arm is endowed with power; your hand is strong, your right hand exalted.

—Psalm 89:13 (NIV)

"The surgery went well." The shoulder surgeon stood at my hospital bedside where I lay, still trying to focus my eyes after anesthesia. I mumbled, "Thank you," but my shoulder already throbbed. What I really wanted was for the doctor to explain how I would get through six weeks in a restrictive sling that bound my arm to my side. My right arm. My good arm. My only working arm.

Earlier, at the pre-op appointment, I'd told the doctor about my predicament. As an infant, I'd contracted polio in one of the final epidemics before the vaccines. My left arm and hand have been paralyzed since then. For decades I relied on my strong right side to do the work of two arms. But now, in late middle age, my overworked right arm suffered major damage. My rotator cuff failed, and a shoulder replacement was my only viable option.

The doctor sympathized with me, but he also wanted the operation to succeed. "You have to promise not to use your good arm for six weeks," he'd warned. Now, recovering from the morning's surgery, I wondered if I could keep that promise.

All afternoon I dozed off and on. The nurses helped me manage pain and assisted me with tasks requiring hands. But as if to torment me in my hands-free condition, my nose itched. I couldn't quite reach the phone or the straw in my water bottle. Suddenly, I felt a compulsive need to scratch, drink, reach phones and do everything else that lay just beyond me. I prayed that I'd sleep until my fingers worked again.

The thought was so ridiculous that I imagined God chuckling but that gave me an idea. If I was laughing, how could I cry? I promptly told the next nurse to place the call button next to my face, so I could press it with my nose. We both cracked up, and I did feel lighter.

As shadows lengthened, I tried to watch TV. An aide arrived with a dinner tray, and after I explained, she spooned bites of pudding into me as I tried to keep from giggling. Hearty laughter made my shoulder hurt, so I politely teeheed. A nurse pinned the call button to the bedsheet near one of my feet and left, leaving my room's door part-way open.

Alone in the dark, I thanked God for getting me this far, and prayed the night would be smooth. But instead of a peaceful sleep, my legs twitched and jumped. With the arm sling and bandages keeping me on my back, getting comfortable wasn't easy. The sling's belt and pillow around my waist chafed and the surgical tape had started to itch. By 2 a.m., I felt trapped and claustrophobic.

To distract myself, I recited the Lord's Prayer over and over. I drifted off to sleep but about 2:30 a.m., I jolted awake with bathroom urges. My toes poked around for the nurse call button, but it wasn't there. Somehow, I'd kicked it off the bed.

Lord, what shall I do? I prayed. Yelling might disturb other patients, and my room was a long way from the nurse's station. I had no idea when the next nurse check-in might be. But what if I could get myself up? The bathroom wasn't far—all I had to do was roll off the bed.

I'd aim for getting out on the side with the bedrail down. I scooted my backside toward my target but got tangled in the IV lines. I carefully straightened the lines, not realizing that my head was closer to one side of the bed. I scooted a little too fast and banged my hurt shoulder against the head of the bed. I writhed around, trying not to scream until the pain subsided.

Only then did I see that my feet hung off the opposite side of the bed, while my neck and head were about to dangle from the other side. I was stuck sideways, with no call button and nature calling even more insistently.

Even if I'd been inclined to laugh at my situation, I wouldn't, knowing what laughing can do to a full bladder. I prayed harder than ever, tears welling up. I told myself that the nurse would come around eventually, but I wasn't sure I'd last so long. I started reciting the Lord's Prayer once more—this time aloud.

On the third time round, my voice quavered. In spite of the comforting words, I felt alone and abandoned. The hallway outside my room was dark and empty. My pain meds had worn off and my shoulder throbbed in time with every heartbeat. I was on the verge of hollering. "Help," I said, my parched voice a dry whisper. Nobody was out there.

I closed my eyes and tried to think of how I could get myself off the bed. If I fell, I might injure or compromise my shoulder. But I had to try.

I managed to get my head onto the mattress, just in time to see a shadowy figure out in the hallway. "Help," I squeaked again. "I need help."

A dark-haired woman in a pink housekeeping uniform poked her head in the room. "*Necesitas ayuda?*" I nodded frantically. In broken English, she assured me that she would fetch the nurse. When she smiled, a wave of peace overcame me.

Moments later, a night nurse hurried me to the bathroom, and then helped me back into bed. As she tended to my IV and fluffed my pillow, I told her I was grateful for the housekeeper's assistance. I grinned. "If she hadn't gone to get you, I might have had an accident."

The nurse looked puzzled. "Who are you talking about?"

"The housekeeper—she had dark hair and didn't speak much English. I was stuck sideways in bed when she happened by."

"Ma'am," the nurse said. "The housekeepers don't work at night. They start in the morning." She retrieved my call button from the floor and re-pinned it to the sheet. "Let me know next time you want to get up."

The next six weeks would be tough, but now I was up to the challenge. When you're helpless, God can hand you confidence you didn't know you had.

The nurse's shoes squeaked as she walked out into the hall. I lay back on my pillow, in awe of God's mysterious ways. I fell asleep knowing that God sent me an angel who lent me a hand.

From Uptown Girl to God's Girl

Kimberly Davidson

Therefore, rid yourselves of all malice and all deceit, hypocrisy, envy, and slander of every kind.

—1 Peter 2:1 (NIV)

If you'd walked into my world when I was in my twenties and thirties, you'd see a put-together "uptown girl," projecting a grand sense of confidence and competency. This superficial and deceitful image, which I donned for over two decades, was a carefully crafted illusion.

There's a saying in psychology that goes, "Genetics load the gun; the environment pulls the trigger." One particular experience, at seventeen years old, I believe squeezed my trigger. Growing up, we ate together as a family every night. One evening, as I reached for seconds, my dad snatched the platter away from me and growled, "You can't have that. You're fat!" I couldn't argue with him; I'd put on quite a bit of weight. Typical of a hurt and rebellious teen, I grabbed the plate, made an insolent face at him, then scooped out a second serving. "I'm not fat!" I declared.

Dad barked, "Get out the scale. I bet you weigh 150 pounds!"
Outwardly defiant and inwardly crushed, I walked away
from the table. *If my dad thinks I'm fat, then everyone else
does.* My dad never had a clue how devastating his remarks
were. How could I not feel inferior, inadequate, and full of
shame? He was my daddy and my rock.

What my dad never knew is that his critical remarks sent
me down a slope into decades of self-criticism, shame, insecu-
rity, and an immense need to be in control. I didn't feel good
about myself, so—to please my dad and myself—I chose to
lose weight. What started as a diet ended up spiraling into
a twenty-year battle with bulimia and other self-destructive
behaviors. I abused cigarettes, diet pills, and diuretics; I
ingested massive doses of laxatives because I believed the lie
they'd make me skinny. *If I'm thinner, life will be perfect; Dad
will be proud of me; I'll be a success and get a husband. Then I'll
finally live happily ever after!*

Ed—my Eating Disorder—became my life. Bingeing let me
detach emotionally from my self-hatred and crappy life by
eating loads of food and then purging it all. Yet, it didn't stop
the cycle of shame and pain.

I gave in to another demon—alcohol. I convinced myself
I was just a social drinker out to have fun . . . and find a
husband. I'd deliberately get drunk and hook up with guys
who just threw me away. My desire to be loved, touched, and
held—plus my lack of self-worth—created a big red flag that
men could quickly manipulate. I deluded myself into thinking
sex would connect a guy to me, that he'd "be there" for me if
I gave him what he wanted. I believed the lie that if I had a
man, I wasn't as worthless as I felt. I dreamed of settling down

with a good, successful husband but, feeling dishonorable, I settled for anyone who would look at me.

It was only a matter of time before something traumatic happened. In college, I was gang raped at a party. Years later, I found myself pregnant from a one-night stand. The solution seemed obvious: abortion. And I was arrested for shoplifting and driving under the influence, went to jail, and got fired from several jobs—piling on more and more shame.

The turning point in my downward spiral came from an unlikely source: the personal ads. Looking for my prince, I had literally answered hundreds of personal ads, only to be gravely disappointed. Then I saw one from a guy named Dennis. It was a humble ad; no overtures of "see how great I am"—which I knew from experience meant "how fake I am." He lived nearby (always a plus in Los Angeles), so I decided to answer it. He called me, and we talked for about an hour about our likes and family, then decided to meet. He was ruggedly handsome and a gentleman. However, he was ten years older than me, so I decided not to pursue his invitation to meet again. I changed my mind a week later, to which he said, "I knew you would." We clicked.

Dennis was a committed Christian, and he wanted me to go to church with him, so to please him I said yes. At Dennis's suggestion, I watched a Billy Graham revival on TV. As I watched, I was drawn to every word Dr. Graham spoke. He then gave his world-famous salvation call. I specifically remember him giving an invitation to TV viewers, asking them to walk up to their screen and touch it as their way of saying, "I accept you, Jesus, as my Lord and Savior." I didn't know why I was drawn to the call then; now I know it was

God pulling me away from my old life and into a new one. The sky didn't open and the angels didn't sing at full volume, but I knew I did something that pleased God . . . and Dennis.

By the time I went to church that Sunday, my heart was beginning to open. I felt I was in a good, safe place. For months, every time the pastor gave the salvation call, I would accept—to make doubly sure I was saved. Later I learned once is enough.

The turning point in my downward spiral came from an unlikely source: the personal ads.

It wasn't too long after that I realized Ed had disappeared. That urge to *obsessively* binge and purge, numerous times a day—for over sixteen years—ended—*boom—stopped*. When I chose to fill in my "binge time" with something productive, like sewing classes, the miracle happened.

At first I didn't realize what a miracle it was. I was going to church, building a life with Dennis—who would become my husband—and had rediscovered my own urge to create through sewing clothes and learning different kinds of arts and crafts. I thought that it was a combination of all these positive influences, combined with my own willpower, that changed my life so dramatically. And yet in other ways, things stayed the same: even though church and faith were part of my life, I wasn't taking the time to really get to know God the way I should. Maintaining my polished "uptown girl" image still felt crucial to my survival. I continued to drink alcohol to excess because the drunk "uptown girl" had a lot more self-confidence and boldness. I also found myself buying increasing numbers of stylish shoes and clothes. It was clearly a case of "musical addictions." I had the beginnings of an ulcer, so I weaned myself off my daily wine. I didn't give God a whole lot of credit because I really didn't know Him and the power He had.

It was only years later that the national disaster of 9/11 (2001) happened, leaving me feeling shaken and spiritually vulnerable. I recommitted my life to Jesus and began to grow spiritually. I began reading the Bible and had a deep yearning to know my heavenly Papa more than anything else. Through this commitment to Him, God genuinely transformed me into a "new creation" and changed my identity. I began to truly believe that *I am worth something—I am loveable—I am enough just the way I am!*

Only after I had become spiritually stronger and wiser did God reveal to me His miracle—my miracle. One day I read a professional article about recovery from eating disorders. It said something to the effect that the recovery rate for a person who has had an eating disorder for more than ten years is about 1 percent. Clinically speaking, there was no solid explanation for my sudden turnaround. Ed was a disease, not something I could have overcome on pure willpower.

That's when I felt God speak into my heart, *You see, my daughter. It was I who released and freed you from Ed; not you.* In that moment, I felt a closeness to my Father that is indescribable. Convinced of God's immense love for me, I took

His hand and received the most amazing life do-over. Within the next year, I completely quit drinking alcohol to excess. That urge had also disappeared.

When I asked Jesus into my life after 9/11, a radical transformation occurred. I dedicated my life to Him and before long was enrolled in seminary. Yet the effects of my past sin didn't immediately disappear. A long road of emotional recovery stood ahead of me. A large part of my transformation process involved healing my damaged emotions. As I healed, God opened doors to new relationships and opportunities—and ultimately, I became a "wounded healer," helping other girls and women with eating disorders.

I can't imagine how different my life would have been if I hadn't seen that personal ad, if Dennis hadn't invited me to church, if I hadn't realized, years later, what a miracle of healing God had performed for me. Now I know that no matter how far away from God we may seem to be, He is always capable of rescuing, redeeming, and restoring those who belong to Him. Once, my life was captive to my past and defined by destruction, but God kept pursuing me and I am now captivated by Him. Today my life is devoted to helping others experience the forgiveness, freedom, and healing I received.

God's Gift Card Provision

Tina Wanamaker

For I do not mean that others should be eased and you burdened, but that as a matter of fairness your abundance at the present time should supply their need, so that their abundance may supply your need, that there may be fairness. As it is written, "Whoever gathered much had nothing left over, and whoever gathered little had no lack."

—2 Corinthians 8:13–15 (ESV)

I stood looking at the inside of our refrigerator, wondering what we were going to do. There wasn't much left in it. And not much in the cabinets either. My husband had warned me two weeks before that the monthly paycheck he was about to deposit was short due to not getting holiday pay and an illness. We would only have about half as much money as we normally would to buy groceries and gas. My response had been, "Well . . . let's just trust the Lord."

And now, here we were—where the rubber met the road, so to speak. I had bought what I could with what we had and there was no more money left for the remaining two weeks of the month. Our refrigerator was almost empty and our cupboards sparse, and there were four mouths to feed, not including my husband and me. As I hesitated at that open fridge, anxiety swelled within me.

And then something else grew even larger and eclipsed it. Faith. I closed that refrigerator door and said, quietly but resolutely, "I choose to trust You, Lord."

I strode out to the living room where our four children were gathered, waiting for our morning Bible time. This was a part of our daily homeschool routine. After I sat down and opened the Bible to 2 Corinthians 8, we prayed together and I began to read aloud, pausing intermittently to ask questions and make sure everyone understood what we were reading.

As we read through chapters 8 and 9, the idea of giving and receiving stood out to us. When we had extra, we could give. When we were in need, the body of Christ could share with us. We discussed this at length and talked about what that could look like for us as a family. The discussion was deep for the ages of the children—ten, seven, five, and three. In our concluding prayer, we asked that God would provide for our need and that He would somehow use us to bless someone around us. We acknowledged we didn't have anything financially to share but that we did have an extra pair of shoes or a sweater, and asked God to help us to be a channel of giving on His behalf.

We finished some other lessons after this, and then the kids were done with homeschool for the day. I began to pick up the house while our oldest son went out to collect the mail. It was a beautiful day and the sun was streaming through the windows. He took his time in the sunshine and came back in with a letter in his hand. "Mom, here's something for you."

I took the letter. It was addressed to me, but the return address was odd. It simply said one word—*Faith*. Wondering what it was all about, I slit open the envelope and pulled another envelope from within. Inside that envelope was a folded piece of paper containing a receipt and a gift card to a grocery store.

The timing was too perfect: The Bible reading, the prayer for provision, my decision at the refrigerator door to trust God. I began to weep in gratitude.

I stared at the gift card in my hand, then looked back and forth between the envelope and the card. The timing was too perfect: The Bible reading, the prayer for provision, my decision at the refrigerator door to trust God. I began to weep in gratitude. God had come through once again. Over and over, time and again, He had shown His faithfulness to us. The choice we had made years ago for me to quit my career and stay home had been right, but also had yielded financial challenges. In these challenges, God had shown His hand many times . . . and today He had done it again.

The thought occurred to me that I should place the card back in the envelope and have our older boy open it. I did that and he opened it and realized what it was. He acknowledged that God had provided for us, that we had received. I sat the kids down and we thanked the Lord for what He had done.

After all of this, I thought to look at the receipt that was in the envelope. It had the amount of the gift card, the store where it was bought, and the date of the sale. The date caught my eye and brought me to tears again. The gift card had been bought on the day that my husband had called and told me we were to be short for that month. But that card wasn't mailed until later, sent so that it could arrive at just the moment when we needed it most.

God's timing is impeccable.

That gift card ended up being just enough to get the groceries we needed for the rest of the month with careful shopping. I smiled the whole time I was waiting in line at the grocery store to check out with that card. The checkout clerk heard all about God's faithfulness as she rang me up, and I practically danced out to the car.

But that wasn't the end of the prayer we had made that morning. It was a desire of our hearts that we could be used as a channel of blessing to someone else—that we would be a part of the giving. The day after all this happened, I received a message from a friend. Her husband had torn his last pair of work pants and they had no money to buy more. She asked me to pray with her for God's provision.

That same day I had a lunch date scheduled. At the end of our meal, it seemed right to share my friend's prayer request with this woman and ask her to pray as well. She looked across the table at me and said, "I can do better than pray." Then she reached into her purse and pulled out a one-hundred-dollar gift card to a clothing store in town. Handing it to me, she said, "Give this to your friend."

Again I held a gift card demonstrating God's provision in my hand. A card that came only from Him. After this lunch, I hurried to my friend's house and dropped off the card, telling her this was from God to her.

The Lord had answered both of our prayers, bringing people together in just the right time and way to assure that everyone's needs were met. He allowed us to practically see 2 Corinthians 8 and 9 in action: Giving and receiving. Needs being brought to Jesus, submitted under His authority, and being provided for in ways we never could have anticipated.

A Late-Night Knock

Darci Werner

*As soon as they saw it, they were astounded;
they were in panic; they took to flight.*
—Psalm 48:5 (NRSVUE)

The knob to the back door rattled but refused to open as I lay trying to sleep. Since my family moved to this small town where my husband was the new police chief, slumber never came easily. Our home had been egged, our lawn burned, and now a late-night turning doorknob as someone tried to seek entry. Was I hearing things? Was I just being paranoid as I tensed up with that same nagging fear that gripped my mind every time he worked the night shift?

I made a quick phone call to my husband, and he headed home to check it out. Pulling into the dark alley beside our house, he found our neighbor's car with the door flung open and a stranger sitting inside. Failed attempts were made to convince my husband that this was his vehicle as he raised hands adorned with blue latex gloves.

Amid a misty rain and poor lighting that cast black shadows around the sheds, safety was a priority. Alone, my husband directed the man to move away from the car and get on the ground. Both of them waited for assistance from a nearby department. As standard protocol, backup arrived, and the would-be thief was taken to jail.

A few days later, my husband received a phone call from the car thief expressing his contempt for the situation. He threatened our young son and me in retaliation. He had a bad reputation in the community, and we were advised to take the call seriously. From then on I traveled everywhere with a mace stick and a bag full of fear—a backpack of anxiety that penetrated to my core and that I was unable to remove.

A few weeks later, I was awakened by thundering pounding on the same back door. *Not again!* Was he back? Was he here to follow through with the recorded threats while it was just me and our son sleeping soundly upstairs?

When I didn't respond to the relentless knocking, the doorbell began to sound. Frantic beating on the door alternated with bell ringing. Every part of my body tensed and breathing became a chore as I reached for the hidden gun and the cell phone by the bed and dialed 911. "There's someone beating on my back door," I whispered to the 911 operator when she answered. My mind was so overcome with fear that I didn't even hear the response.

I rounded the corner to enter the kitchen, holding the gun pointed toward the door. I kept repeating the words "Jesus, help me" as the pounding got louder and louder. My hands squeezed the grip as each breath became more difficult. Each step across the white cold laminate felt as if it was in slow motion as my gaze fixed on the darkness behind the door.

Then it all stopped. I was no longer in control. A calming peace overwhelmed every part of my body. Muscles relaxed and air entered my lungs once again. Ears no longer heard the repetitive banging as I moved calmly toward the door. I was a marionette, trusting the puppet master who choreographed each move. I had no control over my movements as I laid the cell phone on the counter—the line still open and recording every knock and word spoken—and casually tucked the handgun behind my back. I reached for the doorknob and peacefully welcomed our late-night guest.

It was our ten-year-old neighbor. Through tears, he told me he was fleeing from gunshots in his home just a block away. He thought his mother was still alive, but he didn't know where she was. He'd climbed over a deceased family member and run in the dark to a trusted place—our place.

I knew his fear. I knew the panic in his eyes and the grief on his face as he cried. Mine had just been replaced with flowing peace and a calming sense of God's control. It was now my turn to take the blessing just offered me and provide that same grace to him.

I led him to the top of the stairs and into our son's room; our son stood there, frozen in fear, not understanding the circumstances. All three of us watched out the window, where I reassured them of the mighty power of God and the human forces that were doing all they could to find our young neighbor's mom. Red flashing lights lined the streets, mixed with white beams from officers' flashlights, while more vehicles appeared as off-duty state officers signed back on to aid in the search.

As the boys watched the street scene, I made another call to my husband to let him know that our neighbor was safe in our home. He in turn shared that the boy's mother had been found and was also safe. Then came another knock at the back door. It was our neighbor's grandparents, who had come to pick him up and take him to his mom.

When I feel anxious, in moments when I cannot function due to fear, I find comfort in God's leading, knowing that He pulls the strings. His provision includes everyone, from those who serve to protect along to someone who can provide a hug and hold you until the storm passes. There is always a door to knock on for entry, for exit, for movement, or for closure. God provides peace, comfort, and protection every day, not just during stressful times.

God's Mysterious Ways:
Listening through Fear

An accident. A natural disaster. A threatening stranger. There are moments when time seems to slow down, when all we can do is hold on and pray.

In this volume we have many stories of God stepping into those moments of danger, sometimes actively intervening to save a person's life or bring calm to a storm of negative emotions.

Is it possible to learn to be open to that loving calm in moments of terror, in spite of events that are moving faster than you can think? Here are some steps to try:

- **Pray.** Has there been a time when you were in great danger, or when you were in danger of letting yourself be ruled by fear? While in prayer, remember those times. Thank God for the times He helped you, and ask Him to guide you the next time the unexpected happens.

- **Seek.** Are there situations where you find yourself reacting from a negative place, be it fear, anger, or another emotion? Are there times when you know it's going to happen? Take a moment to list them in your mind or in writing.

- **Act.** If you know you're going into a situation that scares you, even if you're already praying about it, take a moment. Stop, breathe, and let God take it from you. Practice doing that every time.

- **Reflect.** Is there a pattern in the times and places when you get frightened? Why do you think it scares you? How can God help you move past that fear?

The Accident That Wasn't

Sandy Kirby Quandt

For he will command his angels concerning you to guard you in all your ways; they will lift you up in their hands, so that you will not strike your foot against a stone.

—Psalm 91:11–12 (NIV)

To celebrate my son, Ryan's, upcoming eighth birthday, one weekend in late January the two of us took a four-hour road trip from our home in Maryland to Colonial Williamsburg, Virginia. After two days of seeing the historic sights, watching artisans work, and eating sweet treats, we loaded up the car and headed home.

Once we were away from town, the only traffic on the two-lane road was a flatbed truck up ahead. It labored under its load of metal rods, each one longer than the length of my compact car.

"What did you like most about Williamsburg?" I asked Ryan.

"The swords at the governor's palace. Those things were everywhere."

"I thought you'd say the gingerbread cakes."

"Oh, yeah. I liked those, too." Ryan reached into the bag at his feet. He pulled out a gingerbread cake and offered it to me. "You want one?"

"No, thanks. Guess it's good we bought a baker's dozen."

Ryan shook his head. "That doesn't make sense. There are thirteen cakes. Not twelve. They should call it a baker's thirteen." Ryan removed his knit cap. He placed his new tricornered hat on his head. "Thank you for taking me to Williamsburg. It was fun."

"You're welcome. I'm glad you enjoyed it." I glanced at my son and smiled.

When we got close enough to the truck for me to pass it, I edged over into the other lane. Then I gasped, "Ryan! Look out!"

At the very moment the front of my car was even with the back of the truck, one of the metal rods broke free of the straps intended to keep it in place. I was heading straight toward a collision. If I hit the accelerator to try to get past before it hit, it might go through Ryan's side of the car. But even if I slowed down, I couldn't avoid the projectile. We were caught, with no way of escape.

"God help us!" I prayed desperately, clamping both hands onto the steering wheel. Every muscle in my body tensed. I watched the metal rod roll off the truck. One end of the rod hit the road mere feet in front of the car. When it looked certain it was going to crash through the windshield, I screamed, "Duck!"

I scrunched my head to my shoulders and pressed my side into the door as I watched the rod bounce toward us. To my

66

amazement, instead of hitting the windshield, the rod somersaulted over the roof. I looked in the rearview mirror. The rod flipped end over end once more, then fell to the ground and stopped.

If I didn't have such a death-grip on the steering wheel, I know my hands would have shaken. My muscles ached from being held so tight. I reached a hand to Ryan. "You OK?"

A slight nod. "That was really scary. I thought we were going to die."

"It *was* really scary."

"I thought it was gonna go right through the windshield."

"Me too."

I watched the metal rod roll off the truck. . . . When it looked certain it was going to crash through the windshield, I screamed, "Duck!"

I had prepared meticulously for our trip to Colonial Williamsburg, but there is only one thing that could have prepared me for the accident that wasn't. That preparation began long before I ever put my key in the ignition and turned onto the two-lane road heading to Maryland: A faith in a God who is actively at work in my life, whether I see His hand or not. A belief in a God who arranges events in my life, in this case events that transformed what could have been a horrific outcome into a safe journey home. And most importantly, a belief that God's timing is always perfect, and that everything that reaches me passes through His hand first.

How else to explain the fact the metal rod bounced in front of my car at just the right distance from my bumper, at just the right angle, at just the right speed, to hit the road in front of the car, bounce over the roof, and flip behind it without so much as a scratch?

It was no coincidence. Of that I am certain. It was a God-appointed event designed to bring my son and me closer to Him. For the rest of our lives, we will both remember with gratitude how God miraculously intervened and protected us.

Marrying the Monogram

Virginia Ruth

For I know the plans I have for you . . .
—Jeremiah 29:11 (NIV)

"Would you look at this?" My husband and I had just moved into our new home, and my friend Lisa was helping me unpack our belongings. She held up a monogrammed "S" silver-covered dish.

I started laughing. "I'd forgotten that I even had that dish. My mom picked that up at an estate sale when I was engaged to the other John. After our breakup, I joked that I would have to find another fellow with an 'S' last name. Not only did I find someone with the same last initial, but all three initials are the same—JES—and he also has the same first name, John."

"That is so weird and such a coincidence," my friend said.

Coincidence? I thought. *Or just God using these details to show us His plan?*

In some ways, my whole relationship with my husband was one big, coordinated effort by God, a series of unlikely events only He could have orchestrated.

The first step on our path toward each other came when I was preparing to go to college. I really didn't even know much about Maryland, except it was one of the rest stops on our way to visit my married siblings who lived in Virginia, but a chance mailer from a Maryland school prompted me to explore this unknown state. Ultimately, I decided their nursing program was for me.

During a college worship service, a girl I didn't know stood up and asked for prayer for finding a roommate. As I needed a new roommate for the next semester, I felt the Holy Spirit nudge me to say yes. My relationship with my new roommate, Sue, allowed me to meet a group of Christian friends, some of whom I dated.

By the time graduation came, I already had my plans: I would move to Massachusetts for a promised job at a Boston hospital. On my final night in Maryland, Sue and I gathered with our friends to celebrate our futures. At dinner I met a friend of a friend, and it was "love at first sight." A whirlwind summer romance culminated in a marriage proposal, and I took a job in Maryland instead.

Sadly, the whirlwind romance ended in shambles, leaving me alone in an unknown area of Maryland with no fiancé and with ten months to go in a yearly employment contract. I wondered about my future and why the relationship didn't work. *Why did you let this happen, God?*

One day, my mom phoned. "We're coming down for Christmas."

"But I have to work on Christmas Day," I said.

"Never mind that. Dad and I will be there. We'll have Christmas dinner for you when you get off work. Dad and I will just have to find a church to attend there."

I wondered about my future and why the relationship didn't work. Why did you let this happen, God?

My parents knew I was lonely. That year, Christmas was on a Sunday, and the only Presbyterian church open for Sunday service in addition to the Christmas Eve service the night before was a couple of towns away. My parents went while I worked. When we sat down for dinner that evening, they were very excited about it. "You should check out this church. It's very much like the one from home."

Why not, I thought. I had been looking around for a new church in the area, but I hadn't yet found one that I liked. In the new year I began attending the church, joining the choir and keeping my eye out for any adults my age. I had seen a handsome "older" guy in the back of the church, but it wasn't until an after-church brunch for the adult Bible study that I first met John. I started attending the weekly study.

On paper, there was no way that we should have been compatible. John is a baby boomer; I am a baby buster, born half a generation later. We grew up four hundred miles from each other: he, a Southerner and I, a Yankee. He went to college in the South while I went to a mid-Atlantic school. He returned home after college, while I never returned to my hometown.

He is an only child of an only child. I am the youngest of four of the youngest of four. He grew up with his parents and maternal grandparents. They rarely saw their extended family. I had numerous nieces and nephews, brothers- and sister-in-law, and I was quite close to my extended aunts, uncles, and cousins.

But as time went on and we got to know each other through the Bible study, we discovered shared activities, lifestyle preferences, and values. We began dating, and then married. While my past relationship with the first JES had been swift and superficial, this one was steadily built on a solid foundation.

"Did I ever tell you the story of my uncle and our wedding day?" I asked Lisa as we continued unpacking boxes.

"Uh-uh." She shook her head no.

"On the morning of our wedding, my out-of-state relatives began arriving. My uncle from New Jersey had never been to our church, nor had he met John or any of our friends. When he walked through the front door, he was shocked, 'Ken, what are you doing here?' he asked one of the ushers. Ken was John's college roommate in North Carolina. Upon graduating, Ken's first job was in New Jersey, and he had attended the same church as my uncle and aunt—he even taught my cousin's Bible study group."

"Unbelievable." Lisa replied. "If John had visited Ken when he was living in New Jersey, he might have met you then. Although that would've been weird since you were only nine or ten at the time."

"But that wasn't the only person my uncle knew. He was surprised to see George, too."

"You mean Pastor George, who married you?" Lisa asked.

"Yup. After Uncle Dave saw Ken, he spied George and said, 'George, what are *you* doing here?' My uncle had gone to college with him. They hadn't seen each other since college days."

"To think that if you hadn't been engaged before, you would not have come back to Maryland and met John," Lisa commented as she peered into another cardboard box.

I thought of all the *ifs*. If I hadn't received the flyer about the nursing school and gone to Maryland; if it hadn't been for the relationship that brought me back to Maryland upon graduation; if I hadn't signed a one-year contract to keep me in Maryland after our broken engagement; if my parents hadn't decided to come and visit me over Christmas even though I was working; if I hadn't gone to the church my parents discovered; if I hadn't joined the small group Bible study—I would never have met John.

During all of that time, I questioned God about where He was leading me, but I saw now that He had a plan. As I recounted the various "coincidences" to my friend, it dawned on me that God had been orchestrating my steps all along so that I would meet and marry John.

"Hey, how did this get in here? I just saw this same can opener in a drawer," Lisa wondered as she pulled the brown-handled opener out of the box.

"You may have. There are two. We each have the exact same one. And the same card table."

"Wow." was all she said as she lay the opener on the table next to the monogrammed dish. Just another one of God's amazing "coincidences."

A Prayer and a Policeman

Carol Gimbel

The Lord will watch over your coming and going both now and forevermore.
—Psalm 121:8 (NIV)

I f only I'd had GPS.
But this happened more than twenty years ago, when my stepson was venturing into college. A financial firm mailed a large withdrawal from JR's college fund. The tuition deadline raced toward us at a dizzying speed. Unfortunately, the tuition money did not.

My husband, Steve, a broadcast engineer, was seventy miles away having an unusually difficult time getting a radio station back on the air.

Late August in Oklahoma is a sauna, hot and humid. I'd spent the afternoon planting phlox in my backyard and had just walked into the house when the phone rang. Hot, sweaty, and badly in need of a shower and a glass of lemonade, I answered, assuming it was Steve.

"Hey," I said, "how's it going?"

Silence.

"Hello?"

Silence.

"Steve?"

Finally, a thin reedy voice asked, "Are you Mrs. Holderby?"

Definitely not Steve.

"Yeesss," I said, a bit apprehensive.

"I have your check." He didn't explain.

"Wait—what? You have my what?" It sounded like a scam. Except most scammers don't sound weak and frail. My mind raced. I waited for it to grab onto something that made sense. It didn't.

"I have your check. It's for a thousand dollars. Can you come get it?" After a pause, he added, "I don't have a car."

I blinked. This man had JR's tuition check. How?

"Oh! Where do you live?" I asked, grabbing a pencil to scribble down the address.

He gave it to me, but no directions on how to get there.

"I don't know where that is." I bit my lower lip as I thought.

"It's near 23rd and Kelley," he said.

I gulped. This poor man lived in the most dangerous part of Oklahoma City. Three-fourths of local breaking news happened in that area. I closed my eyes and imagined me, lost and alone, driving through that neighborhood. Looking for a house. After dark. My imagination tried to go farther, but I reined it in.

"I'll call you right back," I said.

"OK." He hung up.

I called Steve. It took a few minutes to explain the circumstances and the man's location. "What if this is a trick to lure me to that house so that . . . So that . . . Oh, I don't know!"

"Carol, you have to get that check," he said.

"Uh—no!" My stomach tied itself in a knot.

"The tuition deadline is tomorrow. I'm on the top of a radio tower in Apache and can't get home before midnight."

I liked him less by the minute. "So, what's your point?"

He sighed.

"My life is worth less than a thousand dollars to you?"

"It's ten thousand."

"Oh!" We had both just placed a monetary value on my life. "Guess I better go."

"Call me the minute you get back. Be careful," he added, as if that was an option.

He ended the call.

I held the phone, suffocated by an avalanche of emotions. I couldn't breathe. But I was tired of being afraid of my own shadow. I taught a Sunday school class for Pete's sake. Did I trust God or not? Evidently not much, but how could I tell my class to have faith in Him, when I obviously didn't?

It was 7:15 p.m. I had two hours to get that check and get out of there before dark. I checked the charge on my cell phone, grabbed my purse, and ran to the car. I didn't put on lipstick or comb my hair, proving that I was an emotional wreck.

As I backed out of the driveway, I glanced at the profusion of pink crepe myrtle blooms on bushes lining my drive— wondering if I would ever see them again.

I did have a game plan. Police patrolled that area, routinely driving up and down 23rd. I would flag one of them down and ask the officer to go with me. But when I finally turned onto 23rd, frantically praying for a patrol car, I didn't see anything. On that whole seven-mile stretch, there was not one—as in none.

I turned off 23rd onto a narrower side street and drove past small houses jammed close together, all in desperate need of repair. And a lawn mower. Groups of men stopped their conversations to watch me drive by. Which I did. Several times. Although I checked and rechecked the address, I could not find the house. The address he gave me simply didn't exist. Meanwhile, daylight was fading fast.

I turned a corner. A squad car was parked in front of where the house should be. The car hadn't been there the other seven times I'd driven by, and it would have had to pass me to get there. It had not. Nevertheless, there it was. I pulled in behind the police car.

"Thank You, Lord," I breathed, as I got out and walked to the driver-side window.

I taught a Sunday school class, for Pete's sake. Did I trust God or not?

The officer, intent on filling out the forms in his lap, didn't notice me.

I tapped on the window.

Startled, he jumped and looked up. His expression would have been the same if my nose had just fallen off my face. Total disbelief. He buzzed down the window.

"What are you doing here?" he asked.

"My husband sent me," I said. I quickly explained my mission.

"Your husband is an idiot," he said.

"Yeah, I get that a lot."

"Are you the woman who called me?"

"No," I said. "I'm the woman who prayed you here." I thought about introducing myself, but realized he had no interest in adding me to his Christmas list. His only concern was getting me out of there as quickly as possible.

He got out of his cruiser. "OK. Get in your car and wait here," he said, as he walked away, "while I go see about the woman who called me." Without looking back, he added, "and lock your doors."

He returned in no time, his brows scrunched in confusion.

"Are you the woman who called me?" he asked. "No," I said. "I'm the woman who prayed you here."

"Nobody was there," he said, almost to himself.

I got out of the car and followed him back to his cruiser.

"Let me see that address." He reached for it as he turned on some contraption near his front seat. "This is weird," he mumbled. "It shows the house is here. But it isn't." He scratched his chin. "OK, let's go look."

I followed him between two houses. We found a tiny bungalow in someone's backyard. He checked the address.

"You would never have found this," he said, knocking on the door.

Hard to argue when he was right.

Three pairs of eyes, big as silver dollars, possibly belonging to very small children, peered through the gap in the curtains. An old man opened the door. He held an official envelope, which he handed to me.

I thanked him profusely.

"This renews my faith," the officer said, as we walked back to the street. "I don't often see people doing the right thing."

He stopped at his cruiser and looked at me. "Get in your car. Lock your doors. Follow me out of here. Don't lose me."

"Thank you," I said. "You have no idea how grateful I was to see you! And praises to God. I really did pray you here."

He almost smiled. "Well, for whatever reason, glad I could help."

He led me back to 23rd then waved me past him. I never saw him again except in my frequent prayers for his safety.

The next day, on their way to Oklahoma State University, Steve and JR arranged to meet the old man at a Starbucks and gave him a hundred dollars.

Steve passed away from leukemia five years later. His death devastated me. I was terrified by a future without him. But this incident taught me that God is worthy of my trust. He holds me in His hand. Always. Because He always has, I could trust Him with my future.

I Can Only Imagine

Kathleen Stauffer

> I lift up my eyes to the mountains—where does my help come from? My help comes from the Lord, the Maker of heaven and earth.
>
> —Psalm 121:1–2 (NIV)

Sitting in the church waiting for the memorial service to start, I read my friend's obituary in the program: *Janet A. Ludwig, age 69, of Rochester, Minnesota, passed away on Monday, December 17, 2018, surrounded by her loving family at St. Mary's Hospital from pulmonary fibrosis.* On the cover illustration, a woman dressed in blood red clings to Jesus, their faces pressed one to another. Jesus, dressed in white flowing robes, holds her tightly in his arms. The painting, *First Day in Heaven* by Kerolos Safwat, had been a favorite of Janet's.

As others settle in pews, shoulders pressed together, I reminisce. I recollect a twenty-year-old Janet with a braid down her back and a toddler's arms wrapped around her bare legs. My husband and I were new teachers, and we had been invited to Janet and John's house for supper. We blended immediately, sharing our growing-up years, her challenges as a stay-at-home mom and mine as a beginning teacher. I considered her wiser and self-assured in a way I was not.

Months later, we helped their family pack a U-Haul with boxes of clothing and minimal household items. A new job was taking them a thousand miles away to the East Coast. Not wanting to express the feeling that I may never see Janet again, I barely hugged her before they started their journey. It was the summer of 1971. She had no inclination that her life would collapse in big and little pieces. I had no idea how our Creator would interact in both of our lives to teach us something—that Creator God who designed skies and seas also designed each of our lives according to His master plan.

A soloist from the balcony sings "I Can Only Imagine." The church is decorated in preparation for Christmas, and I remember the holiday cards and quickly written notes from Janet about a divorce, going back to school, moving to Minnesota, and another marriage. I had been excited about her move closer to Iowa, but knew in all reality I would not be able to see her. Work, children of our own, minimal finances, and new health issues kept us close to home.

Before our time together even became a possibility, Janet's second husband drowned while fishing on the Mississippi River. Then she was diagnosed with multiple sclerosis. On top of all this, she developed panic attacks over not being able to breathe. Would I ever see her? Could I, after so much had happened? How do you reconnect with one who seems to have more misfortunes than anyone could bear?

The sun rose and set. Routine kept us on our toes. Hours rushed by, then weeks, months, and years. My husband's cancer diagnosis pulled us to Rochester, Minnesota, for surgery, appointments, and chemo treatments. In spite of the dire circumstances that brought us into proximity, I was excited to see Janet, who was working as a nurse at the clinic. We settled into a Subway booth in the bowels of Mayo Clinic during her lunch break. Her hair was short and white. Her smile was the same. We connected immediately, as if the decades spent apart were only weeks.

"How do you do it?" I asked, without mentioning her life's circumstances.

"You just do," she replied sadly, but with a peace I did not understand. I could not imagine a life with such difficulties. Never occupied with herself, she always turned the questions back to me. "And you; what about you?"

We connected immediately, as if the decades spent apart were only weeks.

The time together was much too short, and yet even in that brief visit, her perseverance and joy in the face of everything she has been through lifted me up, gave me courage to face my own challenges. Despite the rarity of our visits, Janet had always been that kind of role model for me.

We went our separate ways, and, again, much time passed.

A checkup was scheduled for my husband in Rochester, and I arranged to meet up with Janet. She took me to a quiet place for coffee and a chat. I couldn't help but notice the cane and oxygen unit that accompanied her. With cups of steaming coffee in front of us, a bell above the door tinkled each time a customer came and went, reminding us that there were lives outside our own. A space heater made an attempt to warm our feet.

"How's it going?" I asked. Janet chewed her bottom lip.

"I've been diagnosed with pulmonary fibrosis." The next words came out in broken pieces. "I may not have much time left." The oxygen unit beeped; I involuntarily glanced at it on the floor beside her feet. "I have this fear of not being able to catch my breath, and here I am." She readjusted the linking tube and looked out the window beside us, a reminder of the winter season. The sun was lost in the clouds. We did not care if others saw our tears.

"I may not see you again," she said. "This is progressive. They've told me to get my affairs in order."

We parted, but I could not say goodbye.

Mayo Clinic and its two hospitals in Rochester, Minnesota, serve more than 1.4 million patients each year. Thousands go up and down elevators and walk the many pathways to and from appointments. Family members often accompany them, filling the many waiting rooms, small cafes, and the gym-sized cafeteria. My husband and I had arrived for a routine appointment. I did not let Janet know I would be in Rochester, thinking she had plenty on her mind and not knowing if she was healthy enough. We took the elevator in the Gonda Building, Floor 18, Pulmonology, for my husband's appointment, checked in, and found a seat in the waiting area to people-watch.

An exit door, where patients leave after finishing their appointment, swished open, and there was Janet in a wheelchair pushed by her sister. We rushed to express our surprise but slowed our approach when we saw and felt an air of apprehension.

"Janet! I can't believe this! The timing!" I dropped to my knees beside her chair so we were face-to-face. There were tears in her eyes.

"What are you doing here?" she asked and looked between my husband and me.

"It's a checkup appointment," I replied and wondered if she felt offended because I did not let her know I would be in Rochester. My husband and I had been traveling such a long distance, and our schedule was so tight, that it had seemed impossible that we would be able to connect in that time. And yet somehow, miraculously, here we were.

She nodded reflectively at my words. "I'm supposed to check in at St. Mary's Hospital," she said. "I will not be going home."

All the usual phrases were not appropriate. *See you soon, good luck, wish you the best* were all useless. We backed away with, "You're in our thoughts and prayers." What a blessing to see her in the midst of all of this—or was it? She had always been such a blessing to me, such a reassuring presence in my life even when we weren't physically together. But was she happy to see me, in this moment when she was facing her own end? Or would she rather have processed her grief in private?

Several days later, Janet called using a cell phone and, through the magic of FaceTime, we were face-to-face! In hospice care, she was in a hospital gown and made fun of her bedhead while gasping for air.

"Please come and see me," she said. I felt a bit uncomfortable. I had never lost a close friend to death, and I wasn't sure that I would say the right things, do the right things. But I knew I could not say no.

"I'll be there tomorrow," I replied.

During the hour-and-a-half drive, I considered all the things I should say. How does one comfort someone who is on their deathbed? Arriving, I tapped lightly on her hospital door and walked in. Janet was smiling, of course! This was Janet.

Now I understood: expressing God's grace,
His constant presence in our lives, was
what she needed at that time.

"Sit beside me," she said, and patted a spot on the bed.

Her third husband sat quietly, clutching a few bedraggled flowers, in the corner of the room. During serious minutes, we shared songs and Bible verses. One of them was Bart Millard's song "I Can Only Imagine." I recite to her, "I raise my eyes to the mountains—where does my help come from? My help comes from the LORD, the Maker of heaven and earth . . ." From Psalm 121, it expresses that we do not walk alone during our earthly journey. I told her how much I loved and appreciated our friendship, how much she had meant to me over the years.

I realized during that visit why we had been brought together this last time—why God had reconnected us with that unlikely encounter in the hospital just as Janet

approached her reunion with Him. During our long friendship, I had always been the one who initiated conversations
about faith, and yet I felt that it resonated deeply with her. The
scriptures and hymns that I shared with her during that last
visit would appear again at her funeral. While I'd questioned
what I could say to her, now I understood: expressing God's
grace, His constant presence in our lives, was what she needed
at that time.

She passed before Christmas and celebrated her favorite
holiday in heaven.

Our early and heartfelt connection as young women and
the few times we happened to come together over decades of
time were mostly unplanned and brief. Unplanned by us, but
very much planned in our Maker's divine ways. I give thanks
to God for this. The thought that something bigger than Janet
and me, something bigger than you and me, is always at work
is both a mystery and wonder. Someday, Janet and I will be
together, again, in God's Kingdom—face-to-face—no sufferings,
no sorrows, no coincidence, and love abounding.

"I can only imagine . . ."

Remembering that unlikely meeting in the hospital, and the
moments of grace that came out of it, I now choose to view
others differently, knowing that an incomprehensible God
uniquely positions me to be where He wants me to be, with
whom He wants me to be, and with the timing in His hands.

Long Shot

Bethany Shelton, as told to Marci Seither

*Commit everything you do to the Lord.
Trust him, and he will help you.*

—Psalms 37:5 (NLT)

This was my second mission trip, and I was so excited to be part of the Ecuador team from our church. We had been sending teams for several years and had an established relationship with the missionaries, Steve and Carol, who ran a small camp in a rural area forty minutes from the nearest town. As a nurse practitioner, Carol set up a makeshift clinic to see people who needed basic medical attention. Everyone I met who had been to Ecuador on a mission trip knew Steve and Carol and the important work they were doing.

By age 18, I had studied enough Spanish to carry on a conversation or translate for others. I was ready to serve and I was all in for what the Lord would have me do during this mission trip. Little did I know that serving others would look totally different than what I had anticipated.

Some of those on our team were ready to tackle a construction project; some were setting up a vacation Bible camp; and the rest of us were on a cleanup crew, taking care of an outbuilding and other things that needed to be done. I was on the cleanup crew. Not the most exciting task, but if that was where they needed me the most, I was willing to commit to doing my best.

"This might take longer than I thought," I said when the door opened, revealing the floor-to-ceiling stacks of junk inside.

We went to work pulling out and sorting the contents into piles. Some of the items needed to be cleaned, others needed repairs, and many of the items needed to be thrown away.

"Ow!" I felt a sting on my calf followed by the soft skittering of what I imagined to be a bug or spider making a quick escape down my pant leg.

I checked and, sure enough, there was a bright red spot that radiated heat.

"That doesn't look good," said another woman on the team. "You might want to have Carol take a look at that." I looked around at the crates, discarded paint cans, and broken mop leaning against the corner. The little insect could be hiding anywhere.

I found Carol and showed her the bite. She didn't seem overly concerned. "It could be several different things out here, so let's draw a few lines with a permanent pen around the swelling and redness to make sure it doesn't spread. We can keep an eye on it."

But the next morning the redness and pain had extended beyond the area we had marked.

"I think you might need a shot of cortisone," said Carol when I showed her. "When we go into town, we can stop by the pharmacy and pick one up. Plus, I think we should call your parents in case it gets worse and we need to send you home."

How can this be happening to me? Lord, I came to serve others and now I have a bug bite and maybe I'm going to need a shot?

I hated to act like a baby at the thought of getting a shot. I hated the thought of being sent home even more.

When we finally made the long trip to town, we had places we needed to be and things that needed to be done. One of the stops was to pick up the shot of cortisone so that Carol could give it to me later that evening. I looked at the bag that held the syringe full of medicine and resolved to do whatever was best.

We were busy that day, just like any day at the mission camp. Distracted by our work, I forgot about the bite. When I checked the place where the bite happened, there was still some redness, but it definitely didn't have the same fiery pain I had experienced the day before.

After making the long drive back to the small village and missionary station, everyone decided to turn in while I walked to the first-aid station. The first thing Carol did was make sure I FaceTimed my parents back in the States. Even though I was a legal adult, she still wanted them to know what was going on and be able to talk to me in person. I explained everything, even the fact that I didn't want to get a shot on my backside. They stayed on the call while Carol did her exam.

"Let me take a look at how it is doing now," said Carol before taking the shot out of the paper bag. She lifted my skirt up enough to examine my calf.

"I think it looks better." She sounded surprised. "It's still there, but much smaller. I think we should consider holding off on the shot if Bethany doesn't really need it."

"Whew!" I exhaled, happy with the good report. I could see the relief on my mother's face as well.

The next day I went with part of the team to help with a camp that was located farther out in the rainforest. I was so thankful I was able to keep working without the distraction of my bug bite. It was only when we got back to our base camp at the end of the day that I found out what had happened while we were gone.

"A man came in who had a huge run-in with a bee's nest and had been stung all over his face and neck," Carol explained. "He was definitely having an allergic reaction and it was getting worse fast. They didn't have time to take him on the long drive to town to get medical treatment—but he didn't have to. We used the shot we had picked up for you and you didn't need."

"Is he OK?" I wondered.

"Yes, he is now," she said. "But if we hadn't had that cortisone shot here, I don't want to think of what the outcome could have been."

I had been so worried about being sent home when I had come all that way to serve, but it turned out that I was there to serve in a different way. The Lord used an unexpected bite at just the right time to help someone who was in need. I guess you could say that the chances of having the medicine at the camp when it was crucially needed to save a life was a "long shot"—one that the Lord had in mind all along.

God's Mysterious Ways: God-incidence? I Think So!

So many people have experienced God's hand at work—moving events at just the right time, in just the right place—that some people have started calling these events a "God-incidence."

Have you had one of those? You move to a new town and, in a series of unlikely events, meet someone who turns out to be a lifelong friend. Or a mysterious ailment turns out to be a blessing in disguise, for you or for someone else.

Maybe you haven't had an experience like that—or maybe you have, and you didn't realize it. A God-incidence doesn't have to be dramatic to have a profound impact on your life.

- **Pray.** In your prayer time, thank God for being present in your life. If you feel like He's been distant, or you haven't felt Him at work, ask Him to show you the ways in which He's been there for you.

- **Seek.** Think about the blessings in your life—the things that make you happy, the things that nourish you, the things that make you wake up and say, "I get to do this today!" Trace them back in your memory. How did they come into your life? How did you come to have your home, your family, your community? How many things had to come together in just the right way for that to happen?

- **Act.** Pay attention to the little things that happen throughout your day. If you feel blessed, even in a tiny way, say, "Thank You, God."

- **Reflect.** How have you seen God in your life today?

The Flow Blue "Accident"

Roberta Messner

*You gave me life and showed me kindness, and
in your providence watched over my spirit.*
—Job 10:12 (NIV)

The call came from out of the blue. "I don't know what's come over me," my friend Debbie was saying. "I got to looking at my Flow Blue collection. Something told me it's meant for *you*. Next thing I knew, I was on a ladder gathering it all up."

Debbie's prized Flow Blue? I'd always loved the lore of the blue glaze that blurred or "flowed" from antique Flow Blue. Flow Blue porcelain had originated in the Staffordshire county of England in the 1820s. When the blue-and-white pieces emerged from the kiln with the decorative cobalt patterns smudged—said to be an accident during the firing process—at first they tossed them. Then those pieces were discovered by folks who preferred its imperfect perfection and a craze began, a literal frenzy.

Two centuries later, collectors had never stopped loving it. I loved it as well. Loved it when Debbie discovered a butter pat or cup and saucer or lidded tureen in one of the hundreds of different patterns created through the decades. And her collection was magnificent. Why, a U-Haul would be packed with it when she left this world for heaven!

My heart beat out of my chest. "You cannot do this," I said. It wasn't just that she was parting with it. *Giving* it to me . . .

Debbie's tone was hushed. "I can't explain it, Roberta. It's supposed to be *yours*. I'll use my Blue Willow china. I brought it in from the outbuilding, and it's sitting here in the living room in Rubbermaid tubs. It's all ready to go in my corner cupboard." I heard a gentle chuckle filled with pure nostalgia. "After all, Blue Willow *was* Aunt Bee's favorite pattern. If it's good enough for Mayberry, it's good enough for me!"

Debbie and I had been friends for years, had long swapped "stuff." Little treasures we snagged at estate sales or thrift shops. When she had a hankering for my antique clock, it was hers without a thought. When she dragged a set of vintage lamps out of an antiques mall on one of our jaunts, she caught me admiring them in her trunk. "I *thought* those would match your new wallpaper," she said. "They're yours!"

But Debbie's Flow Blue was different. How could I accept such a gift? Leave her with the far less valuable Blue Willow? Once more I heard the smile in her voice. "It's meant for *you*, Roberta."

As dog-tired as I was from a day at the computer, her words pulled me toward her cottage in the country. Her voice had been insistent. "You have to come now. It's blocking the path to the bathroom."

The entire drive over, I argued with myself in my head. *You can't possibly take her Flow Blue. What if she regrets it down*

93

the road and she doesn't tell you? Then a more convincing voice. *But you* must!

Debbie had used the beloved Flow Blue porcelain at her other house. At her new place, the simpler, subtle patterns she'd collected seemed lost against its white walls. My log

---

Once more I heard the smile in her voice. "It's meant for you, Roberta."

---

cabin walls were busier, didn't need as much pattern. Meant for *me*, her friend who adored it, too, but was a frugal devotee. The only Flow Blue I owned was the $5 gravy boat I'd picked through a yard sale to find.

I arrived inside Debbie's back door to claim my prize. But I was suddenly so weak, I fell onto the trash can by her washer and dryer. I hadn't felt the best all day, but I was on a deadline and too busy to pay much attention.

Debbie hurried to see what was wrong. "You're all swollen!" she cried. "Short of breath. You look just like my mom when she went into kidney failure. You have to get to the ER!"

She was exactly right, not only about the symptoms but about the cause. I made it to the hospital in time for my condition to be reversed with no permanent damage. But if she hadn't had that sudden urge to give me her collection, hadn't insisted that I come right away, I might have been at home when I realized I was sick, might not have made it back to the hospital in time.

These days, when I admire a piece of my Flow Blue, I don't see the accidental beauty of the blurring of blue. Only the clarity of God's care. I love to turn over a teapot or an egg holder and examine its maker's mark. Ponder the hidden mark known to God and me . . . the Hand that guided it all. It assures me that no matter what troubles me—even if I don't know I'm in trouble—God's protection is ever there.

It is my refuge and my strength. Always. In all ways. In deeply personal ways I could never dream. The creation of Flow Blue china may have been an accident. But the way that my cherished collection of it came into my life? That was no accident.

Near Abduction in Broad Daylight

Liz Gwyn

*God is our refuge and strength,
an ever-present help in trouble.*

—Psalm 46:1 (NIV)

P ort-au-Prince, Haiti, has a history of violent crimes. Groups of street criminals hide in ditches or grass and wait for vehicles in stopped traffic, commonly at traffic lights. They will storm the vehicle and attempt to open the doors. If they are unable to open the doors, they may break the windows or shoot at drivers to render them helpless. These criminals target their prey during heavy rush-hour traffic. Rachel and her friend gained firsthand experience of this one day as they traveled home from work in heavy traffic.

On July 23, 2012, Rachel and her friend Monique left work and were on their way home. Rachel was looking forward to the celebration of her sister's birthday that evening. Her mother was caring for Rachel's six-month-old baby and had given Rachel a list of things to pick up at the grocery on her way home.

Rachel considered the fastest way to get home and decided that her usual route gave her the best hope of avoiding Port-au-Prince's infamous heavy traffic jams. As she made the decision, an unusual feeling came over her. She had a sense in her spirit that she was being told not to take her usual way home. But, not wanting to risk being late on her sister's special day, she pushed the feeling aside and set off on her normal route.

Along the way, Rachel had to visit three different grocery stores to find the items on her mother's shopping list, going slightly out of her way to stop at the third before heading home.

Rachel maneuvered in the heavy traffic. She was especially careful because she was driving a brand-new Hyundai Tucson, an SUV she had just purchased. Then the traffic came to a complete stop. Rachel saw a man in the intersection walking in her direction. He put out his hand and yelled authoritatively, "Stop!"

At first Rachel assumed the man was law enforcement directing traffic, but then she noticed that other cars were passing by her, which struck her as odd. When she looked back at the man, he was pointing a gun straight at her. Still confused and thinking he was a policeman trying to protect her, she looked to her left side to see if he was aiming at someone else. No one was there. She looked back and saw that the man was directly in front of her, and the gun was pointed directly at her head. She was too stunned to react.

Suddenly there was a thump on Monique's window. The man with the gun moved toward the driver's side window and started yelling at Rachel, "I will blow your head off!" Monique started panicking and screaming. A second man approached Monique's side of the car and somehow got the door open. Monique did not have her seat belt on, and the man easily jerked her out of the car and threw her in the back seat. He forced her to kneel down on the floor with her head down while he kept his gun pointed closely at her head.

The other man shook the gun in Rachel's direction, yelling, "Get in the back!" and calling her foul names. Rachel was secured by her seat belt and was holding tightly to the steering wheel. She told herself, *I am not going anywhere with them tonight. I am going home to my daughter. I will be home and sleeping with my daughter.*

Then a third man came and pulled open Rachel's door. He attempted to force her into the back of the car with her trapped friend. Rachel held a death grip on the steering wheel, knowing if he succeeded, she would be kidnapped, maybe murdered. *Lord, are you really going to give that pain to my family?*

At that point, an authoritative voice rang through her mind. *Take your hands off the wheel.* She obeyed, though she was unaware where the voice came from.

The orders kept coming, simple and strict, as if from a military commander. *Put the car into park.* Again, she obeyed.

Take off your seat belt. Steadily, she unbuckled the belt and let it fall to the side.

Lean toward the man. Rachel started leaning toward the direction of the man on the right of her. *No. The other man.* She leaned to her left. *Now, duck under the guy's arm and get out.*

Could she make it? The space was so small it seemed impossible. Making the decision to trust the voice, she was about to reach for her purse when the voice said, sternly, *Don't!*

Steeling herself, Rachel slipped out of the car. The man who had been beside her became confused and slid into the seat in her spot. Rachel stayed calm, running to the back of the car, but there she paused. Her friend Monique was still in there.

The man at the front of the car realized Rachel had escaped. A look of disbelief was quickly replaced by hatred. "How did you get out?!" he screamed. "How did you escape?" Their eyes were locked to each other. He lifted his gun and shot straight at Rachel.

A look of disbelief was quickly replaced by hatred. "How did you get out?!" he screamed. "How did you escape?"

The military voice spoke again: *Just run!*

Rachel started running in a zig zag pattern. Her attacker shot again. She could feel the wind from the bullet as it passed by her head. She ran faster! She saw a parking garage with an armed guard at the gate. She ran to it. She thrust herself to the floor of the garage.

Then the reaction finally hit her. The focus she had during the incident started fading and she panicked. She was falling apart. The guard ordered her, "Woman, be quiet!"

The man who got into the driver's seat when Rachel escaped had been shot by a stray bullet. Monique took the opportunity to escape during the chaos and ran in the opposite direction of Rachel. The first gunman jumped into the driver's seat of the car and tried to leave. He lost control of the car as the vehicle moved in a reverse direction instead of going forward. It was as though something was pushing the car backward. The car ran right into the parking garage where Rachel was hiding and then hit the wall, knocking it down.

The men got so scared they jumped out of the car and started shooting into the air. The parking garage security guard took off running from the scene, and Rachel ran after him. The driver managed to put the car into drive and sped away with it.

Rachel saw a small shop with big iron doors and ran toward it. She heard, "Oh, no! The lady is coming. Don't let her in!" Before they could close the door completely Rachel barreled in, pushing them aside.

"Please. let me use a phone!" Rachel cried desperately. The people would not give her a phone. "Please, just give me ten cents to make a call," she pleaded. In unison, they yelled, "Get out!"

A bigger crowd started gathering around the little store. Then a man walked up to her, asking, "What is your name? Do you know the people who did this? Who is your family?" After getting the gist of Rachel's story, he said, "Here is my phone. Call someone to pick you up." She promptly called her uncle, who lived in the area.

The police pulled into the store driveway and took Rachel with them. While Rachel was at the station answering questions, Monique arrived. She had also been able to get some help, calling a friend who then took her to the police station.

The officers soon realized that the two women were describing the same incident.

One of the police officers said, "Wow. You ladies are blessed. Do you know how many kidnapping cases we have? And you don't have a scratch. Do you know how many people would like to have your luck?"

"Not luck," Rachel answered. "This is grace."

The officers finished taking their report and Rachel and Monique went home to their families.

The next day the police department called Rachel. The officer asked, "How did you escape?"

"I heard a voice telling me what to do," Rachel responded honestly.

"Do you pray a lot? Does your family pray a lot? You are blessed. Whatever you are doing, keep doing it. Do you know how many people would love to be in your position?" He paused for a moment and continued, "Rachel, it is an honor to meet you. You are truly a blessed person. This is truly a miracle."

Ever since then, Rachel celebrates July 23 as her second birthday. She ponders the miracles God did for her. She gets to be a part of her daughter's life. She knows that if her baby had been in the car with her that day, she would not have gotten out of the car. They would both have died.

Rachel feels the key message she can share with others from this horrible experience is that you need to have faith even in moments of crisis. "Do not panic. Tell yourself you will get out. You will get through this. When God is speaking, you must listen."

Stranded

Denise Margaret Ackerman

For my soul trusts in You; and in the shadow of Your wings I will make my refuge, until these calamities have passed by.

—Psalm 57:1 (NKJV)

We made it! As my husband, Jim, guided our truck and camper through the majestic corridor of pines, a euphoric feeling flooded over me. We treasure our annual Memorial Day camping trip to Rollins Pond Campground, located in the six-million-acre Adirondack Park of northeastern New York. Inhaling the soothing pine-scented air, I breathed out the stress of the trek. Ever since we had left home four hours ago, we had shared the winding country roads with a parade of like-minded travelers seeking to get away for the weekend. Between the rush of last-minute shopping, packing for the trip, loading everything into the camper, and then towing our camper through heavy traffic, my nerves were frayed. I was anxious to set up camp and begin to de-stress.

Deep in the park, we finally reached our designated site. Unfortunately, the sharp angle of the driveway could only be accessed from the opposite direction. We headed up a steep hill to the bathhouse parking lot where Jim could safely maneuver a turnaround. My excitement rose. We would soon be setting up camp! I pictured our cozy camper, situated perfectly on the campsite with an unobstructed view of the rippling pond . . . our lawn chairs drawn close to the crackling fire . . . relaxing and soaking in the serenity . . .

CLUNK! My daydream abruptly ended when a loud noise shook our truck.

Jim and I looked at each other. This could not be good. We were in the middle of the steep parking lot. Jim turned the steering wheel to no avail. After putting the gear shift into park, he got out of the truck and climbed underneath to assess the problem. The steering control bolts had snapped off. Our truck wasn't going anywhere—and that meant neither was our camper.

We pulled out our cell phones, praying there'd be enough reception to make a call. Thankfully, the bathhouse was located at the highest point in the park, and one of the only locations that had cell phone coverage. Our first call was to our roadside service. The operator regretfully informed us that our plan would not cover towing in this case because we had a camper attached to our truck. Next, we called the campground's maintenance office in hopes that they might have tools, parts, or some suggestions for our rescue. The befuddled look on the handyman's face as he examined the disconnected steering gearbox confirmed our worst fears— the broken bolts were unusually large, and not something that the camp garage would have on hand. "You're sure lucky you didn't break down while you were driving," he commented.

His statement gave me a completely different perspective as I imagined how much worse things could have been. If our truck had lost its steering while driving through the congested traffic, on the remote wilderness roads, or on a hairpin curve, we could have been faced with a life-threatening situation. Yes, we broke down, but it was in a parking lot with cell phone reception. I whispered a prayer of thanks to the Lord—although we were stranded, we were OK. The handyman provided phone numbers for local repair shops, but they were all closed for the holiday weekend.

Running out of ideas, we decided to call our son, Mike, an automobile mechanic, to see if he had any suggestions. Thankfully, Jim reached him right away.

"All three bolts are sheared?" Mike repeated once Jim had explained the situation.

"Yes," Jim said, "and the small auto repair shops around here wouldn't have bolts that large in stock, even if they were open."

"Dad, you're not going to believe this, but when I talked with my friend, Andy, last night, he told me he's getting ready to send his pickup to the junkyard."

"Uh, that's great, Son," Jim said, "but how does that help me?"

"Andy's truck is the exact same make and model as yours!" Mike's enthusiasm was contagious.

"Seriously?" Jim asked, relief flooding his voice. He looked at me and smiled.

Mike continued, "I'll give Andy a call. I know he'll let me have the bolts before he scraps the truck. And if they're in good shape, I will bring them up tomorrow morning."

"Mike, that would be awesome! You're a lifesaver, Son!" Jim exclaimed.

After Jim ended the call and recounted the details of his conversation with Mike, I breathed a sigh of relief. Our getaway wouldn't be a disaster after all.

As the sun set and the sky grew dark, we climbed into our camper—still attached to our broken vehicle on an incline in the parking lot—to call it a day. Rather than settling in for a restful evening beside a crackling campfire with an idyllic view of the water, we tried to relax in the slanting camper while watching vacationers pull up to the bathhouse for evening showers. Our hearts were filled with a different kind of rest that night as we gave thanks for God's perfect timing and provision. Not only did He protect us from having an accident, but He also had a plan to repair our truck.

We gave thanks for God's perfect timing and provision. Not only did He protect us from having an accident, but He also had a plan to repair our truck.

Morning arrived with a cool mist blanketing the still campground. We were greeted by the music of joyful songbirds and warming sunshine—and, a few hours later, the welcome sight of our son arriving with the much-needed parts. My heart swelled with pride watching him skillfully work, without power tools or fancy equipment, to piece our broken truck back together. The heavy bolts from Andy's vehicle fit perfectly.

By noon, we successfully completed the U-turn we had attempted the previous day. We hugged our son and sent him on his way back home. Jim backed the camper onto our little slice of heaven and unhitched the truck. Like seasoned pros, we went through the steps to personalize our spot—rolled out the awning, spread the welcome rug, and covered the old picnic table with a red-checked tablecloth.

Once settled on our perfect campsite we gave thanks, assured that none of the incidents had happened by chance: breaking down in a safe location, cell phone reception, and the exact parts we needed—provided free of charge! We spent the remainder of Memorial Day weekend enjoying the beauty of God's creation and marveling that God's watchful care and miraculous provision had guided our entire journey.

The Blue House

Linda H. Summerford

*And we know that all things work together
for good to them that love God, to them who
are the called according to his purpose.*
—Romans 8:28 (KJV)

"Come here! Come here!" I called out to the little girl. I had worked late that day and was on my way to a doctor's appointment. I knew I was already running behind schedule, but I couldn't ignore what I'd just seen: a little girl walking alone on the sidewalk. Hair stood up on the back of my neck. I knew immediately that something wasn't right. A girl that young shouldn't be wandering around alone.

"Come here!" I called out to her again, frantically motioning my hand for her to come to my car.

School traffic had died down, so there weren't many cars on the road. She came running across the road into the median where I had pulled over. I opened the door and told her to get in. She didn't hesitate. Tears ran down her cheeks as she climbed into my car.

"Why are you out walking alone? Where are you going?" I tried to question her without letting her hear the fear in my voice. I'd just picked up a five-year-old little girl whom I didn't know. If she'd so trustingly gotten into my car—the vehicle of a complete stranger—what might have happened if someone with bad intentions had found her first?

"My day care driver dropped me off at dance and drove away." She sniffled. "The doors are locked, and no one came to open them. I was walking to find my daddy's office. He works in a blue house. I think it's that way." She pointed her little finger to the back of my car and struggled to breathe as she continued sobbing.

A blue house? That sounded like the place where I worked. "What's your name, sweetheart?"

"Ashley." Her voice cracked through her tears.

"OK, Ashley, what's your last name?" I gasped when she answered. It was the same place. My office was on the first floor, and her daddy worked on the second floor. I recognized the name, although we'd only met a few times as we passed each other in the halls.

I turned my car around and took her back to my workplace, hoping that her father was still there. When I walked into his office, holding the hand of his little girl, he almost fainted.

"What are you doing with my daughter?" He ran to her and looked at me, wide-eyed. I shook my head, explained what had transpired, and wiped my own tears.

"This is a God thing for sure." He thanked me and gave me a big hug.

"I'm glad I worked late today! God had me right where He needed me!" Who else could have ensured that I would be in just the right place, at just the right time, to keep a little girl safe?

It wasn't the last time I would meet Ashley. When she was about ten years old, she attended vacation Bible school at our church. When it came time for the invitation, she raised her hand and made her profession of faith in Jesus. Years after that, I ran into her again at a restaurant, where she recognized me and asked me if she could give me a hug. "My daddy just told me the story of how God used you in my life—that day you picked me up from dance class. He said, 'She's your guardian angel!'"

God uses us in His providence to do His work here on earth. He puts us just where we need to be for Him to intervene in circumstances we don't even know are coming our way. There are no coincidences for the child of God.

The Right Call

Alice H. Murray

*Call unto me, and I will answer thee,
and show thee great and mighty things,
which thou knowest not.*

—Jeremiah 33:3 (KJV)

Slamming down the phone, I forcefully exhaled and scowled. I'd made it clear to my clients that this was a time-critical situation. *How is it possible that they're not answering?* After seven calls to seven different numbers without connecting, I began to think perhaps they had dropped off the face of the earth.

Months earlier this delightful couple, a youth pastor and his wife, arrived for a meeting in my law office. After experiencing infertility and spending much time in prayer, the couple felt God leading them to pursue the option of adoption. They sought my assistance as an adoption attorney in locating a baby to adopt.

Eager to become parents as soon as possible, the couple wanted to make sure I could contact them should a potential situation arise. To that end, they left me numerous contact numbers—their cell numbers, work numbers, and home telephone number as well as the home numbers for their parents.

I chuckled. *Pigs would fly before I wouldn't be able to connect with these clients.*

A short time later, our office received a call from a woman who had just given birth. She felt the adoption option was best for her child and wanted to make the necessary arrangements before her discharge from the hospital. Given these circumstances, time was of the essence. While the birth mother talked, my mind raced, thinking the youth pastor and his wife would be a perfect match.

After obtaining information from the birth mother about her requirements for adoptive parents, I was sure this was a match. Everything she requested lined up with this wonderful couple. Oh, happy day! Well, at least it was until I tried to call them. And I tried, and I tried.

Not reaching either spouse on their cell phones during a business day did not seem odd to me since they both worked. I then left a message on their home phone, anticipating a return call later in the day. But time was passing quickly, and plans needed to be made for a baby placement.

I called the church where the husband worked. The church secretary informed me the youth pastor was out, but she assured me she would pass along a message to him. A church secretary wouldn't lie, would she? I reached the wife's voice mail at work and left a message in a tone indicating the need for an *immediate* return call.

The minutes ticked by without any response from any number I had tried so far. Out of desperation, since I really wanted this couple to receive the placement, I attempted contact with their parents. Answering machines took my calls, forcing me once again to leave a message stressing the urgency of the situation.

Finally, I had no choice but to locate another family for the placement. *Why, God? Why would you allow this wonderful Christian couple to miss the opportunity to make their dream of becoming parents come true?*

Ultimately, another couple received this little bundle of joy from the hospital, and I put the frustrating lack of response behind me. But I did think it was odd that the youth pastor and his wife *never* called me back about my messages—not even to acknowledge that they'd heard from me.

One day the husband called my office. In a cheery voice, he informed me he was taking his church youth group to Disney World for a long weekend. The purpose for his call? I needed to have the number for the hotel where the group was staying—"just in case," he explained. I bit back a sarcastic comment and refrained from mentioning the previous possible match or his lack of response. *It's not likely anything will happen over the weekend anyway.*

The next morning, God got the last laugh. Once more our office received a call about a last-minute baby placement. Again, I thought of this couple; honestly, they were the top candidates for receiving a baby even if their track record for returning phone calls left something to be desired.

I called the hotel and asked for the youth pastor's room. A sleepy young male voice answered and asked me to hold. The youth pastor, who was sharing a room with some of his charges, came to the phone and found out he could expand his family if he desired. Boy, did he!

Hustling to get the baby placed with the new parents, I had little time for chitchat with the couple. When things calmed down, they sat across from me in my office one day beaming

112

from the joy of having a baby to raise. "This match seems to be the perfect one for you," I commented. "It's a good thing you didn't respond to any of my phone messages about that previous last-minute placement."

The couple raised their eyebrows and frowned, turning to look at each other. I realized from their expressions that none of my previous attempts at contact had gotten through. They hadn't even known about the other baby. But how, when I'd called so many different numbers and left so many different messages?

Smiling, the husband explained they'd told God they only wanted the baby He had in mind for them. They asked that He not let them even hear about any adoption opportunity He didn't mean for them. And they hadn't.

All my unreturned calls to this couple were more than a series of technical malfunctions. This couple didn't get any of my messages, but they certainly received God's message loud and clear—the other baby was not His plan for them. When it was God's time, they got the right call.

God's Mysterious Ways: When God Doesn't Call

The stories in this volume are all about times that God showed up in people's lives in unexpected ways. But what about times when you're sincerely seeking God's help or guidance, and you don't seem to get an answer?

Ruth Stafford Peale, wife of Guideposts founder Norman Vincent Peale, once wrote, "God always hears our prayers, and He does respond to them, but His answer may take one of three forms: 'Yes,' 'No,' or 'Wait a while.'" Our perspective is so limited compared to God's. Sometimes what we think is best turns out not to be. And sometimes now is not the right time to move forward.

It may not be possible to know for sure, but there are ways to be more open to the answers:

- **Pray.** If you've been asking and asking God for something in prayer, try changing your approach—ask Him to show you if now is not the right time, for example, or to help you understand what you *should* be asking for.

- **Seek.** Keep an eye out during your day for little things that might be an answer to your question.

- **Act.** If you do get a sign that you should be looking in a different direction—follow it!

- **Reflect.** Think about times in the past when you prayed for or about something, and it seemed like your prayers weren't answered. What happened instead? Were there blessings in the way that things did go?

Stopped by an Angel

Toby Williams, as told to Ellen Fannon

*You're safe not because of the absence of danger,
but because of the presence of God.*

—Jeanette Windle

The day had started out like every other weekday. Getting my five children, ages nine to fifteen, ready for school—and myself ready for my job as the principal of the private Christian school they attended—could only be described as carefully controlled chaos. I finally had all the children rounded up and seated in our recently purchased Chrysler Town and Country minivan. We headed down the street with me drilling the kids, as usual.

"Do you have all your homework? Do you have all your sports equipment? Do you have your band instruments? Do you have your lunch?" The kids assured me they had everything they needed while talking, laughing, and pestering each other.

I pulled up to the red light at the intersection of our street with the main highway into town. The light had probably just turned red, as I was the first vehicle. *Great. Now I'll have to wait for the whole cycle.* I drummed my fingers on the steering wheel while my mind buzzed with all the things I had to get done that day.

Finally, the light turned green and I stepped on the gas to make the left turn. Nothing happened. *What in the world?* I looked down to be sure my foot was on the pedal. It was, but the van wasn't moving. This was a new vehicle that had never given me a problem. Perplexed and a little frustrated, I pumped the gas again, but still nothing happened. *What am I going to do? We're going to be late.* To make matters worse, this was back before cell phones, so if the car wouldn't move I couldn't even call for help.

"Mom, the light's green!"

"Go, Mom!" called my helpful children from the backseat.

I still had my foot on the pedal when suddenly a speeding eighteen-wheeler ran the red light on the main highway perpendicular to us. He didn't attempt to stop or even slow down. My heart skipped several beats and plummeted to my stomach. If we had been in that intersection, he would have hit us broadside and crushed us, probably killing us all. I don't think the driver was even aware of the near disaster he had just missed. This sequence of events probably took less than five seconds, but it is seared forever in slow motion in my brain.

I sat for a moment as I steadied my shaking hands and tried to wrap my mind around what had just occurred. All I could do was say over and over again, "Thank You, Jesus. Thank You, Jesus."

When my pulse returned to normal and I could think somewhat clearly again, I stepped on the gas pedal. The van moved forward as if nothing had ever been wrong.

Still shaken by this experience, I shared the incident later that night with my husband. It had to have been God's hand at work, I told him. Angels had surrounded us, keeping us safe.

"We'll take the van in to a mechanic tomorrow and have it checked out," he said.

"But it's worked fine since this morning," I argued.

"I still want to be sure."

The next day, my husband took the van to a trusted mechanic, a member of our church who owned a vehicle repair business. He ran a thorough check on the van and could find nothing wrong with it.

"Sorry," he said. "Everything is working normally. I can't explain it. I don't know what to tell you."

My husband and I exchanged glances. "We know what happened," I said. "There's only one explanation."

We have shared this story many times over the years as a testimony of God's divine protection, and I still get tingles every time I think about how close we came to disaster and how God stepped in to save us. It makes me wonder how many other times God has intervened in our lives that we never knew about.

God's Perfectly Timed Text

Juliette Alvey

*For he will deliver the needy who cry out,
the afflicted who have no one to help.*

—Psalm 72:12 (NIV)

Island life has its advantages: the weather and natural beauty of Hawaii are hard to beat. There were times when I would look around at my surroundings and ask, "Lord, how in the world did I end up here?" We had the privilege to *live* in a place where most people feel lucky to visit for a week.

While we were thankful that my husband, Ryan, was called to serve as a pastor on Oahu, we quickly learned how isolating it can feel to have over two thousand miles of ocean separating you from friends and family. The rapid turnover of people (and surprisingly, this was not exclusive to the families of the personnel assigned to one of Oahu's fourteen military bases) made it challenging to develop deep relationships. Many people who lived "on island" long-term tended to keep others at arm's length for this very reason. If someone is going to move away in the next year or two, why risk the heartbreak of gaining and then losing a good friend? This isolation was one of the many factors that led our friend Mary into a hard place.

Mary and her new husband, who was in the Navy, visited our church two times. Ryan met them and exchanged information, but for some reason, I missed them both times. I had three young children to run after, so I was probably occupied at the playground during coffee hour.

Some weeks passed and they hadn't been back at church so, as he typically tries to do, Ryan checked in with them to see how they were doing. He had Mary's number, and one day he decided to text her. Mary replied in awe of the timing of this text. At that very moment she was in the psych ward at the military hospital after checking herself in the day before with suicidal thoughts. It turned out that her husband had a drinking problem and would become angry and violent. She started to live in fear of the one person close to her on the island, the person who was supposed to be taking care of her. With no family nearby and nowhere to go, she thought about ending her life. Her love story had turned into a nightmare, and she couldn't go on. Mary had a background in psychology and knew the warning signs. She could diagnose one thing for herself: she needed help.

Ryan went to visit her in the psych ward to hear her story and pray with her. He came home from that visit with a strong feeling that we needed to do something to help this young woman. Usually he keeps his visits with people confidential and doesn't involve our family in other people's struggles. But he was convinced God was telling him that this situation was different.

The next time Ryan went to visit Mary at the hospital, he brought me with him. Only one person could go in at a time, so I went in first. Mary had on blue scrubs and was sitting in a sparse room that was probably being supervised by one of the health professionals. It felt strange to meet someone for the first time under these conditions, but the more we sat and talked, the more natural it felt. Even though it was awkward, Mary and I bonded in that little hospital room. This dire situation that she found herself in tore down walls, and in this vulnerable state I could see her, a fellow child of God in need.

When we got home, Ryan and I discussed the ways that we might be able to help Mary. We didn't have much money—island life is not cheap!—and we couldn't think of many ways we could help her situation. But we had a home. It seemed like all she needed was a safe place to be until she could get things figured out. So we invited her to come stay with us, and she gladly accepted our offer.

We were living with three kids in a three-bedroom house, so we moved all of the kids into one room and gave Mary the third bedroom. I had no idea how to picture what it would be like having her stay with us, but it was a risk God was leading us to take.

Mary cut ties with her husband after her hospital stay. Although he tried to text her occasionally while she was with us, it was clear that she would have to build a new life for herself. She was under a lot of stress—having to figure out how to move forward, applying for jobs, seeing counselors, and even having a few health issues—and yet she was a joy to be around. And even though we had set out to help her, in the process, she became such a blessing to our family.

For me, having her present in our home made me feel more accountable as a parent—in difficult situations where I might have lost my patience, I tried to stay calm and speak to my children in a more loving and patient way. But the timing was even more fortunate for my husband.

Mary did not know at the time (nor did anyone else besides me), but Ryan was really struggling in his ministry. He felt that his time there was coming to a close, and that God was calling us to go somewhere else. During the time that Mary was with us, I was secretly grieving the fact that we would probably not be in that beautiful place for much longer. Our situations were more alike than she realized because we, too, were feeling uncertain about the future. But when we thought about Mary, we had a very personal reminder that we had at least one good reason for being there (although I'm sure there were many that were more difficult for us to see).

Even though we had set out to help her, in the process, she became such a blessing to our family.

On her end, aside from having a safe place to stay while she got back on her feet, Mary had a special bond with each of our kids, and I think they were helpful in her healing process. Our youngest had recently turned one, and I remember Mary snuggling with her on the couch, with eyes closed and taking deep breaths. There is not much in this world as calming and healing as a baby sleeping on your chest. It was a special time for her to be with us because it was when our little one started walking. Being present for these little milestones made her feel even more like part of our family.

What an amazing blessing that God allowed our stories to intersect at that time and place on that isolated island away from family and friends. I believe that God used us to rescue each other, and because of that, we became lifelong friends with Mary. It's even more astounding when we think that it all happened because of a text message. It's frightening to think of where she might have ended up if Ryan had ignored that seemingly random impulse.

Mary is now happily remarried, has a baby—who I am sure gives her plenty of calming and healing snuggles—and is involved in prison ministry. We will always remember those three short months that we had together and will continue to think of her as family. Thank God for His amazing and perfect intervention!

Miraculous Distractions

John Smith, as told to Mindy Baker

Trust in him at all times, you people; pour out your hearts to him, for God is our refuge.
—Psalm 62:8 (NIV)

As our plane landed, I felt excited for what the next few days would hold. My co-workers and I planned to visit five remote villages in a country where evangelism is strictly forbidden. Mission work in the countries I travel to is a privilege and a calling, but it is not without risk. As a representative of an organization that works in the least-reached regions of the world, I often hear from the leaders I train about the persecution they endure for their faith in Jesus Christ. The goal of our trip was to see firsthand the work of the local men who had been using our disciple-making strategies. We had done extensive training with these leaders, but this would be our first opportunity to witness the growth of their house churches and meet the new believers face-to-face. Although risky, we had video equipment with us in order to document the ministry for a report to our donor base.

It was mid-afternoon by the time we passed through customs and security and loaded up two vans with all of our luggage.

The drive to the first site was both arduous and memorable. The scenery was rugged and rural and the terrain rough. We bounced along the dirt road, urban civilization a distant memory. When the road came to an end, we parked in a pasture and walked a short distance to a primitive village with thatched huts built around the edges of a large open space. Brightly colored laundry dotted the landscape, both hanging from ropes and draped over poles. Curious children peered out of their dwellings, at first too shy to emerge.

My nose detected an agricultural smell; cow patties had been stuck to the side of the huts to dry in the sun and later be used for fuel. Chickens and other barnyard animals roamed freely, noisily welcoming us to the community. Large bunches of green bananas recently harvested sat leaning up against a cement retention wall, and tarps were spread on the ground in the central area in preparation for our arrival.

Word spread that we had come, and soon many members of the small community gathered to greet us. They sat on the ground and offered us plastic lawn chairs. We watched as the worship began. Some played the drums as voices praised the one true Creator. Their faces expressed the meaning of the words they sang. It was obvious that they loved Jesus with all their hearts, souls, and minds. Material wealth was not what brought them happiness; it was knowing their sins were forgiven and their eternal destiny was heaven.

After a time of praise, we heard testimonies of their faith, translated into English, as many people wanted to share how the Lord had changed their lives with people who lived outside their village. We videotaped those testimonies, thinking about how encouraging the footage would be when we shared it back home. None of the believers seemed worried about the presence of the video camera. After the service, the village held a feast that included chicken, rice, and vegetables. They gave us sugar cane to gnaw on and then offered a tour, ending at the hut that would be our bedroom for the night. Our beds were boards that we covered with sleeping bags, and we set up our mosquito nettings.

None of the believers seemed worried about the presence of the video camera.

In the morning we woke up and traveled to a second destination a short distance away.

The second village had a very similar appearance to the first, and we watched a second simple church service seated in the same type of plastic lawn chair. We had the video camera out in plain sight and captured more footage of the precious testimonies, each one translated by a trusted local believer. Nothing seemed risky or dangerous. One of the villagers excitedly told us of plans for a ten-by-ten hut to become a twenty-by-thirty-foot space for the believers to gather together in worship.

We traveled on to a third location and parked our vans near what looked like army barracks, not realizing their significance. A path had been cut along the side of a rice paddy and palm trees stood towering above other lush foliage. After twenty minutes of hiking, we reached a clearing which was a third village. Little did we know that our presence in this remote location was so unusual that it had attracted unwanted attention. Once again we witnessed a church service, shared refreshments, and videotaped testimonies. At one point, a young man leaned over and pointed out that there were two strangers present in the community. I noticed that the strangers were taking pictures of us, but I didn't feel concerned or worried. I later realized I should have.

After the third meeting, we casually walked back to our vehicles. To our shock and surprise, the border patrol stood waiting to question us. Apparently, the third village was very near the border of a neighboring country. That was why there were army barracks. It also became clear that we did not have the appropriate permits to be in this area. The serious body language and tone of voice that the guards used put me on high alert as my mind strained to remember all that I knew about how to handle this type of situation.

The guards marched us to the middle of a field. They told us to sit down. We sat. They told us to stand up. We stood. They took our passports. They began to ask us questions. The same questions. Over and over again. First one guard, then another.

They made us stand out in the field for hours, with multiple guards taking turns questioning us. In between our interrogation sessions, they did a great deal of consulting with one another while we stood wide-eyed, hearts pounding, silently beseeching God to help us.

What will happen next? Will they arrest us? Will we be allowed to go back to our hotel? Will we get our passports back? Will they allow us to come back into their country for future trips? As the leader, I felt responsible for the other group members. My mind raced, searching to discover a way out.

126

I had two main fears. First, that they would scrutinize my passport closely. I am a frequent traveler who often goes to unusual locations. I felt my passport would raise suspicion and further jeopardize our safety. My second fear was that they would discover the video equipment.

I knew it was extremely risky even to have the equipment, but if the guards discovered the footage that we had taped while in the villages, not only would we be in danger, but so would the local church members. I began to cry out to the Lord in prayer. *Please do not let them discover the video equipment. Help us. Please protect us in this situation.*

The interrogations continued. "We are here because we love your country and we want to see it," we said over and over. "We are fascinated by the beauty of your culture and the people. Anyone can go to the tourist sites, but we want to see how the people really live."

They began to methodically search each bag. I started to sweat profusely as they got closer and closer to the bag with the equipment.

When a guard finished questioning us, another one would begin with the same questions. Hours passed and I found myself surprised that they hadn't searched our bags yet. I began to believe that perhaps they wouldn't.

My hopes were dashed when they began to methodically search each bag. I started to sweat profusely as they got closer and closer to the bag with the equipment. But as the video bag was being opened, the man doing the search miraculously received an order from a superior that sent him on an errand. To our amazement, the man did not return to his search, and the video equipment was never discovered.

I thanked God for that first miracle and begged Him to do it again. *Please let the guards return our passports without an issue,* I prayed fervently.

As it began to grow dark, the chief of the local police arrived. His intimidating presence was powerful. He sauntered over to our huddle holding the stack of passports. In front of us, he opened each one and questioned its owner. My body was tense, and my nerves on edge. My passport was the last one. As he lifted my thick passport to thumb through it, his cell phone rang. He answered it and began talking excitedly, mindlessly turning and handing the passport back to me without a word. I could barely believe what had happened.

"Thank You, Lord," I whispered, my heart somersaulting with joy.

After what seemed like an eternity, the first group of guards returned, this time asking us political questions, both about our president and about their prime minister. I felt a prompting from the Lord to speak.

In a firm voice, surprising myself with my confidence, I said, "We have been here all day. We would love to answer any of your other questions, but we need to get back to our hotel."

And with shocking ease, they agreed. In an instant, our all-day ordeal ended, and we were allowed to load up our vans and leave. Just like that. We were speechless.

As we drove back to the hotel, we rode in silence. Our minds relived each harrowing moment, yet our hearts praised

God for His divine intervention and our miraculous release. Although disappointed that we were unable to visit the other two villages—we were scheduled to leave the area the next day—our experience filled us with extreme gratitude and joy. We discovered that day that God truly does work wonders in our modern world.

One Small Mistake, One Amazing Gift

Michelle Stiffler

And this same God who takes care of me will supply all your needs from his glorious riches, which have been given to us in Christ Jesus.
—Philippians 4:19 (NLT)

When my four children were young, we lived 5 minutes from my parents' house. My middle sister lived equally close most of those years, and our little sister was still at home, finishing high school. It was an ideal situation, to be sure, making spontaneous movie nights, ice cream outings, or leisurely dinners on the deck easy to coordinate. We all attended church together and holidays were a no-brainer—prepare a dish and gather at Mom and Dad's.

My little sister was last to get married, but first to move away. Her military husband was stationed across the country, so a week after their wedding, they were packed and gone. A few years later, my husband and I moved our family of six cross-country, too. It was an enormous transition, as expected, but I took comfort in our trips back to Virginia, where a sense of "sameness" was preserved for my children. Our old church was there, my sister's house was there, and of course, my parents' house—with the red door, flower beds, and lush green yard—was there, just as my children remembered.

Five years after our move, my parents shared their plans to move as well. I was happy for them, but as I processed the imminent transition, I also realized the imminent loss. My parents were moving from the only home that had remained constant for my children, the one place where permanence, belonging, and nostalgia were safely kept. This sentiment fueled a desire to make one trip back to my parents' house—for my kids, for my parents, and for me.

As summer turned to fall, the desire became a longing for one last Thanksgiving in my parents' house with all of us together. My youngest sister had already made plans for her family to spend Thanksgiving in Virginia, so it wasn't outside the realm of possibility. The trouble was, I'd been seeking answers for a health issue, and plane tickets for my family of six didn't fit into our budget. I began praying the Lord would provide finances for a Thanksgiving trip. I trusted He could do it, even if I didn't know how.

Life went on. The kids went back to school, and my eldest—a new high school graduate—went to community college. My health concerns were still unresolved, resulting in frequent appointments, blood work, and more unanswered questions. Then, amid a series of routine diagnostic tests, one test came back with a drastic change in values that showed kidney dysfunction, setting off a new round of tests and even more worry and stress.

As I sat on the papered table of the kidney specialist, my shoulders relaxed. I'd waited weeks for this appointment, and very soon, I'd know my next steps. The doctor came in, flipping through my chart. He introduced himself and before I could respond, he asked, "I'm assuming you weren't born in 1878?"

I began praying the Lord would provide finances for a Thanksgiving trip. I trusted He could do it, even if I didn't know how.

"No," I answered, a tad perplexed.

"Well, your birth year was entered incorrectly," the specialist continued, without pause. "This error skewed the formula for calculating your kidney function. Your recent test results show your kidneys work just fine." He reached for the door as I attempted to make sense of the new information.

"So, I don't really need to be here?" I asked, standing to go.

He shook his head. "No need for a follow-up appointment. Your kidneys are in good shape. Best of luck."

I climbed into my car and stared out the windshield before turning the key. For nearly a month I'd been consumed by my health, or seeming lack thereof. One careless mistake had created a whirlwind of emotions and energy, ending with a bizarre finale of relief. I was thankful the worry was over, but I was also frustrated. I'd needlessly wasted time and money I didn't have, all because of an error. Suddenly, I realized what I needed to do. I dialed the number on my lab report and took a deep breath.

After summarizing my situation, the customer service representative quickly offered to correct my lab report. I explained I was calling from the parking lot of a specialist's office where I did not need to be and that amending my lab report would not give me back a month's worth of time and copays. She agreed and connected me with the proper department. My claim was assigned to Brenda.

Over the next two weeks, I emailed receipts and documents to Brenda. She was apologetic and compassionate, but from the beginning, she was transparent that the resolution for my claim would be reimbursement of my copays and nothing more. Whatever time I'd lost, whatever concern I'd carried because of the lab's mistake, was to be resolved on my own. Financial motives hadn't fueled my reasons for contacting the lab—other than recouping my out-of-pocket expenses—but I couldn't resist entertaining the notion that my peculiar experience might be connected to my prayer to celebrate Thanksgiving with my nuclear family. It seemed far-fetched, but what if the lab's one-digit slipup was God's means for providing money for plane tickets?

This notion was put to rest when Brenda emailed the total reimbursement I'd receive by check—just enough to cover what I'd spent on appointments and tests since my lab report with the error. Once the check was mailed, my claim would be closed. The whole ordeal was over.

The next morning, Brenda surprised me with a phone call.

"I woke up in the middle of the night thinking about your case," she said. "I've been in this field for quite some time," she continued. "Claims don't interrupt my sleep anymore, but I couldn't get your situation off my mind. I've submitted a request to have you reimbursed for your time, trouble, and gas money, in addition to your co-pays. It's already been approved, so I'm excited to tell you the additional reimbursement will be . . . hold on, let me find the exact amount."

Earlier that morning, I'd checked the price for six plane tickets to Virginia during Thanksgiving break. The price had gone down to $1,600, but it was still out of reach, and I'd been kicking myself for looking in the first place. "Lord, please," I prayed inaudibly, "Please let her say $1,600."

Brenda cleared her throat. "The check total is $1,680."

My brain and mouth were completely incapable of forming words. Brenda didn't seem to notice. "Again, I'm sorry for the trouble caused by the mistake. I hope this reimbursement helps a little. Best to you, Michelle."

We managed to keep our trip to Virginia a secret from my sisters and parents, resulting in a day spent surprising family members at work, at the bus stop, and of course, at my parents' house. Funny thing is, I don't remember the Thanksgiving meal that year, but every other piece of that trip—the delight, the togetherness, the sheer gift of it all—is deeply embedded in both my heart and my faith. When money is tight or a need arises that is outside my means, I'm reminded of God's unexpected provision. He delights in caring for His children. All we must do is ask, receive, and give thanks.

Remarkable Peace

Renee Mitchell

*And the peace of God, which surpasses
all understanding, will guard your hearts
and minds through Christ Jesus.*

—Philippians 4:7 (NKJV)

The day began like any other. The weather was warm and sunny, almost perfect. I found myself humming as I worked, praising the Father for all the blessings in my life. Our first grandson was due any day, and I was ecstatic, to say the least! The thought of a little fellow being in our home again was keeping me flying pretty high those days.

It was about 5 p.m. or so when my husband decided to change the brake pads on my daughter's Cavalier. When he did that, I liked to grab a lawn chair and sit outside and visit, just in case he needed anything. This day was no different. The birds were chirping and he was singing as he worked, which always made me smile.

After the job was completed, he asked for me to get into the vehicle and pump the brakes, then move the car closer to the garage. I'd done this many times before, and I was comfortable with the task, but this time I didn't pump the brakes enough. The car started to roll backward. I swung the door open to yell at my husband and before I knew it, I fell out and was pulled under the car.

After that, I remember only pieces. My husband coming toward me, waving his arms and frantically yelling, "Stop!" Trying to lift myself up and being pushed back down by the weight of the car. The undercarriage of the vehicle on my face, and then darkness.

When I came to, I was lying against the front tire. My husband and children had pulled me from underneath the car. It had run over my leg and right up the middle of my body. There were ambulances and police vehicles everywhere. There was horror on everyone's face. It was so chaotic, and yet I felt such peace throughout the whole thing.

Then I got very cold and began to shake violently, which I later discovered was a sign I was going into shock. They placed my daughter between me and the tire so she could hold me and keep me warm.

All of a sudden a helicopter landed, beaming a light down on me, and the paramedics began prepping me to be airlifted to a nearby hospital. As they were talking, I heard the paramedic say that they were certain that I had broken my neck, back, and pelvis. I remember thinking, *I must be in pretty bad shape.*

As my daughter held me, I could hear her praying. I could see my daughter-in-law pacing back and forth, and I could hear her praying as well. My son knelt in front of me and told me that I had to be around for the new little one coming and that God wasn't going to let me go.

I refused the helicopter because they wouldn't let anyone go with me, so they loaded me into the ambulance. On the ride there, they missed a curve and we almost went off of the road. As we came to a screeching halt, all of the supplies above my head came crashing down on me. The paramedic made a mad dash and pushed them off my face. I looked up at her. "Do you know Jesus?"

"You need to try to relax," she told me, adjusting my neck brace.

"God is so good," I said. "I know I'm going to be all right."

"You're in pretty bad shape," she replied. "You shouldn't have refused the helicopter." She sounded angry with me, so I decided to lay quietly as requested. During the ride I prayed, and the song "Healing Jesus" kept running through my mind. I knew the Lord was with me and that He had it all under control. A warm blanket of peace came over me, and I felt no pain at all.

During the ride I prayed, and the song
"Healing Jesus" kept running through my mind.
I knew the Lord was with me and that
He had it all under control.

When we arrived at the hospital, they rushed me to the trauma unit. I was met by some very serious and eager doctors and nurses who had obviously been prepped for my arrival. I was turned and twisted every which way and X-rayed all over more times than I can count. I would be lying if I said I wasn't afraid. At some points what they were saying sank in, and I wondered if I would live long enough to hold my grandson. But as those thoughts tried to creep in, the peace that passes all understanding took over, and I felt an overwhelming calm. I told anyone close enough to hear that God had already promised me I was going to be OK. I asked each one of them as they came close if they believed in prayer. "Do you know my Jesus?" I asked. Some would just smile and pat my arm, and others would lean in close and say, "Yes and I know He's with us now." I knew the believers, and I could sense they were praying for me.

> *"Ma'am, we have all agreed that*
> *we are looking at a miracle."*

The next thing I remember, I had two doctors looking down on me. One was a pretty blonde woman with a sweet smile and tears streaming down her face. She leaned over me and said, "Ma'am, we have all agreed that we are looking at a miracle. When the paramedics radioed in, they told us they were bringing in a woman who had been run over by a vehicle and had a broken neck, back, and pelvis, and two crushed legs. We expected that you would be near death and were going to need extensive surgery and care. I was shocked that you were speaking when you came in. And even though we checked you over and over, we found that you didn't have a single broken bone in your body."

They finally let my family into my room. I'll never forget the way they smiled through tear-stained eyes as we thanked

God for the miracle that we all knew He had performed for us. The doctors wanted to keep me overnight, but after much debate they let me go.

The next morning, my family and I went out to the spot where the accident had happened. My husband showed me an indention in the driveway where the car had rolled over me. The police had told him it was like the earth had parted under me, and I was in that space long enough for the vehicle to pass over my body. Had I been lying on asphalt, I wouldn't have survived. I had a mental image of my guardian angel pushing the gravel and dirt away just in time for me to fall in, and I smiled.

I'll never forget that July day or the way God sent just what I needed to survive. A couple of weeks later, I held my grandson for the first time. As the tears ran down my face, I again thanked God for our unmistakable miracle and His protection on us all!

God's Mysterious Ways: The Gift of Peace

In several stories throughout this collection, we see examples of people in the midst of crisis—sick, injured, or struck by financial or personal troubles—suddenly overcome by a sense of peace. It's God's way of telling them, "It's OK. I've got this."

It's impossible to know why sometimes that feeling comes and why sometimes it's so elusive. But if it feels like you can't seem to find God's peace even in your everyday life, why not ask the Source of all Peace to bring more into your life?

- **Pray.** In your prayer time with God, talk to Him about the things that are troubling you. Ask Him to bring peace into your life.

- **Seek.** What are the areas of your life that bring you stress? Make a list of situations and areas that cause you the most worry. Keep in the back of your mind that when those situations arise, you're not alone.

- **Act.** Whenever your troubles surround you, pray for peace. Try to remember to do it whenever you feel yourself overwhelmed by a negative situation.

- **Reflect.** How did you feel after you prayed for peace? Do you find it coming more often?

God Sees

Elsa Kok Colopy

From heaven the LORD looks down and sees all mankind; from his dwelling place he watches all who live on earth—he who forms the hearts of all, who considers everything they do.

—PSALM 33:13–15 (NIV)

I was in so much of a hurry that I almost missed it. I almost missed the moment that left three of us in tears.

It was a Friday afternoon and I had a few extra moments before picking up the kids at school. I had to exchange a shirt at a local clothing store. I picked out the new item and positioned myself in line behind an older woman and her daughter. Just on the far side of the register was another woman waiting with her arms full of clothes. She waved the older woman ahead of her, "I respect my elders," she said with a smile. "You only have a few things, go on ahead."

I smiled at her. Sweet.

At the same time, I glanced at my watch. I only had a few minutes to spare. I tried to push off the impatience dancing in the wings, but I could feel it encroaching on my relatively good mood.

It took a bit, but the older woman paid for her items and headed off with her daughter. The kind woman stepped up to the register. She placed two small stacks on the counter—she was exchanging one for the other.

The cashier calculated it all up. "That'll be twelve dollars difference," she said.

The woman hesitated. "OK, then. I need to put something back."

I don't know what came over me. I jumped up to the credit card machine and stuck my card in. "No, you don't." I smiled big at her.

"Oh no," she said. "You don't have to do that!"

"But I want to," I said. Truth is, I'd been in her shoes and people loved on me. It was my joy to pass it along. I didn't plan it, but my next words poured out straight from the heart. "You need to know that God loves you."

Tears sprang to her eyes, "I can't believe this!" She paused. "Can I please give you a hug?"

"Of course!" I said. I wrapped my arms around her and the words kept coming. "Your God loves you. He loves you and He sees you. He really sees you."

The woman immediately stepped back and covered her face with her hands. She started sobbing. Eventually, she spoke through her tears. "I've been asking. I've been asking God, 'Do you even see me?'" She cried again. "He sees me." She said it in wonder several times over. "He really sees me."

Goosebumps covered my arms. Tears filled my eyes. I glanced at the cashier, who was also in tears as she watched our exchange. "Oh, He definitely sees you," I said. "He sent me here today for the sole purpose of making sure you know that. Everything in me wanted to put off exchanging this shirt because honestly, I hate shopping. But I came anyway. It must have been for you!"

We laughed. "Can we be friends?" she asked.

"Absolutely!" We exchanged numbers and have been in touch ever since. Turns out she's a single mom. I was a single mom. Our daughters share a birthday. She's a writer, I'm a writer.

On my way out, my heart was so full. I was grinning from ear to ear. While I was embarrassed by my impatience and almost missing the moment, I was so grateful that God overruled and helped me to see. I know He could have used a hundred different people to love on this woman. But today, He chose me! I was honored and grateful. And even as I was reminding that beautiful woman that God sees her, something happened in my own heart. *God sees me too!*

Funny thing. I went up to the register and exchanged my item. I received eight dollars back on my card. After paying for her items, that means it only cost me a whopping four dollars to pour love into a hurting heart. Four dollars to remind a soul that she is seen. Four dollars to experience a moment I'll remember for a lifetime.

Best four dollars I ever spent.

When One Open Door Leads to Another

Laurie Davies

Now to him who is able to do immeasurably more than all we ask or imagine, according to his power that is at work within us, to him be glory . . .

—Ephesians 3:20–21 (NIV)

"Would you take me backstage to meet her?" I asked my friend. I tried to remain calm. *I think I sounded too eager.* "Please?"

A musician I admired would be performing at my home church for a one-night women's event. Even though I had spent years practicing with choirs in that backstage room, this was a national tour group. I'd need my friend—who knew the musician personally—to open the door.

I felt awkward asking. This was a newer friendship. But my friend could tell it was important.

"Yes, I'm sure I probably could," she said. "How do you know her music?"

As fast as tears can tumble, mine did. I blurted a string of almost unintelligible phrases about grief, loss, and the lyrics that saved my life. This musician had written the soundtrack of my testimony. She held my hand through a hard, mean season.

I know God is not bound by time, but I picture Him in that moment wanting to speed time along because He knew something I didn't. I wasn't just going to meet a musician when she came to town. I was going to land my dream job.

I couldn't breathe. A significant relationship was unraveling, and it really did seem final. In a strange way, I'd braced for it. But even as I replayed the last, heartbreaking conversation in my mind, I wondered if anyone can really brace for such a thing. My view from the bathroom floor offered little perspective.

I sat on the ceramic tile and sobbed.

Would I recover? Would I even survive?

I had to pull myself together. I couldn't drive into the carpool lane at my son's school looking like this. I washed my face with cold water, put my sunglasses on—the big ones I use for swim meets or beach vacations—and took a deep breath.

"God, I'm going to need everything You've got today," I whispered as I grabbed my car keys and backed out of my driveway.

A song called "Take My Hand" shuffled through my music streaming app. I hadn't heard it before.

It spoke of brave obedience, fallout, and a God who carries us when we can't find our way through the pain. Word for word, the lyrics made sense of my circumstances. I'd never felt so seen by a song.

I think I remember picking up my son at school that day. I definitely remember racing home to download the song. I must have listened to it twenty-five times that night.

I felt hope.

Five years had now passed since that day I crumpled to the floor. I'd kept that simple song in my regular playlist rotation. With each passing year, the lyrics reminded me more about what God had healed than what had been lost.

The event at my church would start in about thirty minutes, and I could hardly wait to meet the artist! My friend opened the backstage door and made polite introductions.

"I can't believe I'm getting to meet you," I blurted to the musician. "Your song got me through the most difficult season of my life. I think you must have gone through something really hard to write those words. Thank you for not wasting it."

Tears flowed. We hugged and posed for a few photos.

I would have been delighted to take my seat in the audience and soak in the rest of the evening—especially since, unbeknownst to me, "my song" had been worked into the evening's set when it wasn't usually performed on this tour.

But God had so much more in mind than I could have asked for or imagined. He had a precision blessing in store. That's my label for what the world calls "luck."

Before the event began, while we were still backstage, my friend went to talk with some of her other friends. This left me standing for a few minutes next to the evening's keynote speaker, an accomplished social researcher and author. Her inviting tone suggested we might share a few words of pleasant chit-chat.

"So, what do you do?" she asked.

"The short answer is, I'm a writer," I said. "The long answer is, I have a mishmash of journalism, consumer medical writing, and vocational ministry experience."

Her eyebrows raised.

"Right now I feel a little unfocused, wondering where I fit into the ministry landscape," I confessed.

The speaker told me she had *just* lost her longtime editor, a ten-year staff member who left to pursue a wonderful ministry opportunity. She hadn't even advertised her newly vacant position yet. We had a hunch God might be up to something as she took a photo of my business card and told me her staff director would reach out.

One month later I joined her team as lead editor.

My hodgepodge of consumer medical writing (often spent in areas like the latest neurological advances), journalism, and vocational ministry experience didn't add up to anything coherent—until I met a researcher fascinated with brain science who needed an editor with a heart for ministry.

Talk about precision.

In the months since I've joined her staff, I've often reflected on that backstage encounter. Some might call it random or even a fluke, but I know better. Only God could connect the dots between my eclectic résumé and a researcher excited to meet someone with exactly that résumé. Only God could broker that meeting through a song I wouldn't have loved if not for the hardest season of my life. Only God could bring a new friend into my life who would open a backstage door so He could throw open a much bigger door.

It's the greatest evidence I've seen in my own life of Romans 8:28, those famous words that Paul penned to his friends in Rome: "And we know that in all things God works for the good of those who love him, who have been called according to his purpose" (NIV).

God works in all things. Even the worst, heartbreaking things.

In the way that only God can, the heartache I was most afraid of led me to a job I could only have dreamed of. This is the intentional hand of a loving, redeeming God. He really does take the painful, loose ends of our lives and tie them into something beautiful.

A backstage encounter on a Friday night in November proves it.

All That I Needed

Penny L. Hunt

Your Father knows what you need before you ask him.
—Matthew 6:8 (NIV)

After weeks of intensive training at the Cooper Institute in Dallas, Texas, I passed all the physical requirements, completed my practicum, and received an aerobic dance instructor certification.

With time to spare before my departure and excited to present my vision of using aerobics to share the love of God with others, the idea popped into my head of doing a "cold call," a sales technique I'd learned years ago. I stopped at a large church nearby. Remarkably, the senior pastor was free to meet with me.

He listened intently with sincere interest and even brainstormed ways for me to communicate the concept with other churches. He liked the idea of using contemporary Christian music in class and encouraged me to end each session with a quiet meditation, including a mini devotion. He said he would share my ideas with the church's pastor of athletic events and asked me to leave contact information with his assistant.

I stood to leave, but he stopped me at the door. "Before you go, I feel impressed to give you some money."

Somewhat stunned, I said, "Oh, no. Thank you, I don't need any money. My flight and rental car are paid for, and I even have an extra five dollars for snacks."

But he insisted and reached for his wallet. "I wish it were more, but I don't carry much cash. Please, take this." He pressed eleven dollars into the palm of my hand.

"This is very kind, but I don't need it."

When it became evident he would not take "no" for an answer, I tucked the bills in my pocket with a submissive sigh of thanks and headed for the airport.

As an inexperienced traveler, I'd left the credit card my husband and I used only for emergencies safely tucked away at home. I departed for my "all-inclusive" training with my handbag filled with sunglasses, tissues, hand cream, and breath mints—but no extra cash reserves.

I'd utterly forgotten the "full to full" fuel policy for my car rental. The fuel tank was full when I picked up the car, and I needed to return it the same way.

Dread filled my heart as I stopped at a gas station outside the airport. I hadn't driven anywhere except to and from the training center, but I could see the gas gauge hovering slightly below full. I anxiously held my breath, squeezed the gas pump handle, and watched the numbers roll upward.

I exhaled with a heavy sigh of thankful relief when—*click!*—the numbers slowed and stopped at *exactly* eleven dollars.

My eyes rimmed with tears at the realization of God's perfect provision, given before I knew I needed or asked for it.

God Towed My Heart to Safety

Linda S. Clare

*He stilled the storm to a whisper;
the waves of the sea were hushed.*

—Psalm 107:29 (NIV)

One December day, the stormiest storm of the year hit my Oregon town with wind and cold rain. I prayed and worried as the rain pelted down. My husband, Brad, was late. Something was wrong.

Finally, he walked in, pale and soaked to the skin. For the past seven years, my husband of forty-five years bravely faced three-times-a-week kidney hemodialysis. His skin was always ashy pale after one of these sessions, but standing there dripping wet, he looked defeated. Our car wasn't in the driveway. My alarm bell sounded.

I grabbed a towel and rushed to help dry him off. "What happened?"

He steadied himself against a counter. "I was rounding the corner down by the school," he said. "The car just died in the middle of the road."

My eyes must have widened. "Died?" I couldn't imagine our old but reliable Honda Civic ever dying.

He shot me a look. "Yes, died. As in no power. I couldn't even get it into neutral to push it to the side of the road."

I wanted to cry, but I hugged him. "Come on, get some dry clothes and stand by the fire. You're shivering."

He shook his head. "But the car's sitting in the middle of the road!"

A prayer was already galloping through my mind. "Go warm up. I'll go to the car and wait for the tow truck."

Before all his health problems, my ex-Marine would have done all this—especially on the stormiest day of the year. But he just said, "You'll have to take care of it." He warmed his hands next to our pellet stove while I bundled up for the walk to the car.

I opened the door a crack. A nice-looking young man in his early twenties stood there. "Do you need help?"

I stepped around puddles and the sticks and leaves blown off trees. I only had to walk about a half mile, but my heart broke thinking of Brad facing the weather after a grueling four-hour dialysis session.

Once I spotted the car I prayed harder and faster. He hadn't lied—the little red Civic sat in the middle of the road. Cars were pulling around it, but the drivers didn't look happy at being inconvenienced.

I walked faster, ducking my head against the wind as I approached the Honda. Just then, a woman driving a white Lexus honked as she made the detour around me and made a rude gesture. I practically leaped inside the Honda, mouthing *I'm sorry* to the driver as she sped off.

I couldn't budge the gear shift out of park. Even the hazard flashers didn't work. Now I was shivering from the cold. I told myself to calm down and breathe, but I was scared and anxious. Only praying for God's help seemed to refocus my thoughts.

I inhaled deeply and thanked God for smart phones as I accessed the insurance company website for a tow. Multiple screens asked me for all sorts of information, and I groaned when they said the tow truck couldn't come for an hour. I closed my eyes and settled in to wait.

I jumped when a knock came at the driver's-side window. The windows were so fogged over that I couldn't see much more than the shadowy figure of a person standing outside. Fearing it was another angry driver, I hesitated. But something told me that help was here.

I opened the door a crack. A nice-looking young man in his early twenties stood there. "Do you need help?" Despite being soaked, he had a warm smile.

I explained that the gear was stuck in park, preventing the wheels from rolling. I shot up another prayer—*thank You, God*—grateful that I was no longer alone. Maybe the young man could at least fend off the irate drivers.

But instead of giving me moral support, he asked, "Do you mind if I have a look inside?" He smelled clean and earthy; a particular piney scent not masked by any artificial fragrance.

These days, you hear so much about people who are out to take advantage of older folks. But I knew that this man wasn't going to hurt me. I got out and he sat in the driver's seat. Without saying a word, he used a key to pry up a small square of plastic next to the gear-shift column. Once it was off, a keyhole appeared. He turned his key in the hole.

I thought I was witnessing a miracle. The young man proceeded to put the car into neutral. He got out and muscled my old car to the side of the road. I was nearly in tears, I was so grateful for his kindness. Right then, the tow truck pulled up, lights revolving, loud diesel engine competing with the howling wind.

I called my husband to tell him the tow had arrived and said I would be accompanying the truck to a repair shop. "I'll call you from the shop and you can pick me up," I said. I couldn't wait to tell him about the man God had sent to help us.

The tow-truck driver got out and began to ask all sorts of questions about where I wanted to take the car and whether or not I'd be riding along. I answered as quickly as I could, eager to get out of the storm and go back to my husband. I was still amazed at the little trick that young man had known to be able to push the car and get it off the road. That tiny square of plastic hid a secret only a car aficionado would know.

I turned to thank the young man who'd pushed my car to safety. He was gone.

I've never figured out who had that magical key and those strong shoulders. But if I ever smell that particular piney scent, I'll know God has sent someone to tow my heart to safety once more.

Six More Months

Wendy Klopfenstein

Be careful for nothing; but in every thing by prayer and supplication with thanksgiving let your requests be made known unto God.
—Philippians 4:6 (KJV)

"See you next week." Mary made a face as she pushed open the door. "If we still have jobs."

As she exited to the parking lot, a cold gust of wind swirled around my desk. Typical of Oklahoma storms in January, the rain outside had begun to freeze. Those dismal gray skies matched the mood at the office. Every employee would go home to a three-day weekend. Before Monday, we would all receive a letter in the mail. The letter told us whether we needed to bother driving to work the next week. In other words, huge layoffs.

In the six years I'd worked there, they'd thrown lavish parties, taken big corporate trips, and offered stellar benefits and pay. No one suspected that behind it all, the company teetered on financial disaster. Until that fateful January. In an effort to salvage the company, they brought in an expert to tighten the budget and turn things around. A cut of about half the workforce was deemed necessary.

As a single mom with a mound of debt still looming over my head from my failed marriage, I took a hard look at my finances. With at least six more months of my current salary rate, I could pay off a couple more of the credit cards with higher interest rates. It would place me in a much better position. I did the best thing I could think to do. I prayed. Hard.

"Lord, You know the situation. You know what another six months' worth of this salary could do for me. If it be Your will, please let me be kept on, but I understand if someone else needs it more. Amen."

I took a hard look at my finances. Six more months of my current salary rate would place me in a much better position. I did the best thing I could think to do. I prayed. Hard.

That prayer had flowed from my lips multiple times, in varying forms, over the past week. All that was left now was to go home and wait.

Saturday afternoon, I bundled up for the trudge out to the mailbox. I pulled out the letter, barely able to wait until I reached the house to discover the verdict. I tore open the envelope the moment I stepped inside.

"Did you get it?" My mother moved away from the sink full of dishes to stand by my side.

I scanned the contents, searching for the words I longed to read. Once I found the long-awaited answer to my prayer, I exhaled. "I'm going back on Monday."

My mother slipped an arm around me as thankfulness welled up inside me.

The next week held an element of chaos as those remaining attempted to fill in all the gaps left by the ones let go.

"Wendy, do you mind stepping into my office for a moment?" My manager beckoned from her doorway.

Once inside her office, I seated myself across from her. She paused, as if trying to think of how to begin. Surely, they weren't changing their mind about my position now?

"I'm asking a couple of the ladies to come back in. One of them will train you on her job."

I marveled. The employee coming back had been my relief at the front desk. She already knew my job. Yet, she was being asked to return for a week to train me on how to do hers.

My manager sighed, as if debating whether to go on. "You weren't originally on the list to stay."

Silence hung in the air. I didn't know what to say.

"In our Human Resources meeting, I asked them what they planned to do about having someone answer the phones." She paused, as if she felt the magnitude of it all, even if she had no knowledge of my prayer. "So, they added your name to the list."

"Thank you." *And thank You, Lord.*

She nodded her dismissal. The weight of those meetings appeared to have taken a toll on her. That and not knowing what would be next. We all felt it.

Over the next few weeks, I worked hard to learn the additional skills needed. With time, the atmosphere began to hold a degree of hope for the future of the company. Surely, things were turning around. Spring rolled by as I continued applying any extra money I had to the balances on the credit cards.

When summer arrived, rumors surfaced again. Rumors that things weren't turning around as the company had hoped, even with all the drastic cuts.

"I heard someone say they are going to file for bankruptcy." A fellow employee hurried to keep pace with me as I made my way to the ladies' room on my break. "They would tell us, wouldn't they?"

I didn't know the answer. "I haven't heard anything."

How did I tell her I wouldn't know if they were planning such a thing? Sure, I worked in the Human Resources department, but I managed the reception desk. The only clue I ever received about big news came in the form of calls from the main office or an increase in closed-door meetings. When I stopped to think about it, I'd seen more of both. But it didn't have to spell disaster.

Later that afternoon, an email arrived in everyone's inbox. Pack your belongings. Turn in your badges. Go home. The company had filed for bankruptcy.

Stunned, I moved in slow motion. I'd been preparing for possibilities, but the reality hit hard. What about everyone who hadn't been making plans, thinking that the company might stay open? I finished packing the last of my personal items. With one last glance at my desk, I pushed against the door leading to the parking lot. Unlike the prior exodus of employees back in January, this time the sun warmed the somber crowd. As I approached my car, a sudden realization hit me. It had been almost exactly six months since the day of my prayer.

God's timing turned out to be perfect in another way: It was just around that time that my family's business suddenly began to boom, requiring more help. As the company I'd been at for six year closed its doors, I stepped back into the family business, learning new skills and supporting their influx of new customers. Twenty years later, my sister and I run the business.

God's Mysterious Ways: The Gift of Trust

Hand in hand with experiencing God's peace is being able to trust God's direction for you. It might sound simple; it might even be simple to say, "I trust You, God." But it's hard not to worry in difficult situations, or not to question what's happening when it seems like everything is going wrong.

Often people think of trust in God in terms of responsibility—if you have faith, you should trust Him, right? But what if trust is a gift? Maybe, like peace, it's something that God can give you, a sense of His presence, a knowledge you can rely on that everything is working toward a good end. We might be reminded of the father in Mark 9:24 (NIV), who said, "I do believe; help me overcome my unbelief!"

- **Pray.** When you have doubts, take them to God. Tell Him what's on your mind, and listen for His answer. What does He say about the ways He acts in the world—and in your life?

- **Seek.** As you go about your daily life, look out for situations that might test your faith or your trust in God. Notice when they happen, and notice how you react to them.

- **Act.** In moments when you find yourself doubting, worrying, or afraid for the future, say, "I trust You, God. Help me overcome my unbelief."

- **Reflect.** Are there ways that *you* can be a sign of God's presence in the world?

The Cruise That Never Ends

Becky Alexander

*I am with you and will watch over
you wherever you go.*

—Genesis 28:15 (NIV)

The first week of the twelve-day cruise was fabulous. Turquoise-blue sea and warm sunshine, buffets and soufflés, steel-drum music and tropical islands. It promised to be the perfect voyage.

In my day job, I'm a tour director escorting motorcoach tours, but twice a year I train other tour directors for the International Guide Academy. This time, the training took place aboard the *Norwegian Breakaway* on a cruise to the Caribbean. Classes took place during hours at sea, while days in port offered students and instructors leisure time to explore. A great gig for me.

The trip from New York City to our first port of call, San Juan, lasted four days. Being out of touch with my family that long made me a bit nervous, because my dad's health hadn't been good in recent months. However, cell phone service aboard ship cost $75 for 100 minutes. I figured that I could talk to them in San Juan, since Puerto Rico was a US territory and covered by my phone plan.

When we arrived, I called my sister, Cindy. "Hello! Just checking in. How's Dad?"

"Well, I don't want to worry you, but he has declined some. He fell twice yesterday and got several cuts and bruises. The home health care nurse is here with him now."

"Oh, no! Should I come home?"

"No," she said. "I'll keep you posted. The doctor made an adjustment in his medication that he thinks will help."

The ship moved from San Juan to Saint Thomas overnight. Following a breakfast of eggs Benedict—one of my favorite cruise treats—I disembarked on the island and rode the Skyride to Paradise Point. It was there, overlooking the harbor, that my phone rang. Caller ID read "Cindy."

"Hi, Beck!"

It was *not* Cindy—it was my dad! I was so relieved to hear his voice, though weak, and his words, though slurred.

"I've got to get out of here," he said. I assumed he meant the bed that confined him. He much preferred a tractor seat.

"You will, Dad. You always do. I'll be home in six days. I love you."

The ship journeyed on to Saint Martin and then Saint Kitts. All the while, Dad grew worse. Shortly after I spoke with him, he suffered a major stroke and slipped into a coma.

My new goal became to get home as quickly as possible. Ship personnel helped me search for flights out of the islands. I would have to take an island hopper here, board another island hopper there, lay over twenty-four hours in San Juan, adjust my flight between New York and Huntsville, Alabama.

Between the many connections and the long layovers, I feared I might get stuck in the Caribbean indefinitely.

If I stayed on the ship, I would be home in four days. That seemed the surest way to get me there in the shortest amount of time.

My new goal became to get home as quickly as possible.

Early the next morning, I stood on the highest balcony of the atrium, feeling helpless and trapped. I prayed for my dad, my family, and my own broken heart. As I stared down on the sparkling decks below me, a man tapped my arm.

"I didn't mean to startle you," he said.

I recognized him as Derek, the man I'd met a few evenings earlier when I sat beside his family in the dining room. During conversation over three delicious courses, we discovered a connection—we both had served as ministers in churches.

I smiled. "My mind was far away."

He continued, "This is going to sound strange, but I saw you while I was eating breakfast." He pointed toward a nearby restaurant's open-air seating. "God nudged me in my spirit to come talk to you."

My eyes filled with tears. "Thank you," I whispered. "I received news from home . . . my dad is very sick . . . he's dying."

Derek threw his arm around my shoulder and right in the middle of a bustling boat, petitioned God to cover me with His heavenly love.

All alone—1,700 miles from home—God provided comfort through a faithful fellow believer.

The *Breakaway* soon docked on the British island of Tortola, our last port before returning to New York City. I needed space to process everything that had happened. So I went ashore for a while and wandered down narrow streets past brightly colored houses.

All alone—1,700 miles from home— God provided comfort through a faithful fellow believer.

My simple map showed four churches along Main Street— Catholic, Anglican, Methodist, and Baptist. I found them all and snapped several pictures. But something intrigued me about the lovely white Anglican church with its red shutters, red handrails, and a red cross above the entrance. I turned the doorknob and stepped inside. Beautiful, peaceful, soothing. I sat on a pew.

"Welcome," a man's voice broke the silence. I hadn't noticed him near the piano at the front.

"Oh, I'm sorry to interrupt you," I said, rising to leave.

"Please, feel free to stay as long as you'd like. We're having a worship service with the children from our school."

At that moment, a side door flew open. Children wearing green-plaid uniforms rushed in and stood next to me, in front of me, and behind me. The man at the piano hit a lively intro, and the kids belted out a song from Psalm 100 with joyful clapping and jubilant dancing: "Enter His gates with thanksgiving and His courts with praise; give thanks to Him and praise His name. For the Lord is good and His love endures forever."

Once again, God comforted my grieving soul—this time through a choir of praising children. It was no coincidence that these children sang about entering the gates of heaven at a time when I was praying about Dad's passing.

Now, if I could only get back home to see him before he left for eternity.

The return voyage through the Atlantic Ocean was nothing short of a blockbuster movie. A storm brought nineteen-foot waves, wind gusts over ninety miles per hour, hundreds of seasick passengers, and a vessel that tossed and groaned for three days. Due to a medical emergency, an elderly man had to be transferred mid-storm into a small boat—the winds were too high for a helicopter evacuation. The *Breakaway* participated in a search-and-rescue mission when the turbulent seas threw a man overboard from a cargo ship ahead of us, delaying us further. And before my heart could reach the shore, I received a four-word message from my sister: "Dad just met Jesus."

The ordeal reminded me of an infinite-loop kids' tune called "The Song That Never Ends." With a few minor adjustments, it became the perfect stress reliever for me while riding in a rocking cabin. "This is the cruise that never ends. Yes, it goes on and on, my friends . . ."

We did, finally, make it back to New York, though half a day late. I wasn't sure if my tears represented grief or stress or exhaustion or relief. Likely, a combination of them all. I missed my flight home and had to spend the night in a Manhattan hotel. But my family delayed Dad's service until I could get there, and we were able to celebrate his life together.

For a long time after that, I didn't want to set foot on another cruise ship. Missing my dad's last moments on earth while trapped onboard has weighed on my mind to this day. Yet because of "the cruise that never ends," I received two extraordinary gifts—two divine encounters—that proved God's presence in my life and assured me of His ever-close comfort, no matter how far I roam.

The next year, I was offered another teaching gig on a Caribbean cruise. Knowing God would travel with me, I accepted it.

Blind Faith

Leah Vidal

*We know that all things work together
for good for those who love God, who are
called according to his purpose.*
—Romans 8:28 (NRSVUE)

My sister and I sat huddled together in the back seat of a rental car outside the hospital where our mom had been admitted less than twenty-four hours earlier. Between tears, we prayed to God for a miracle.

All we wanted was to be with Mom, but lingering COVID regulations were still in place at this hospital. A strict security guard positioned at the ER entrance was turning family members away, pointing at the posted sign: PATIENTS ONLY. We had tried to enter the hospital only to witness an elderly woman in tears being separated from a young man who looked to be her grandson. Her tears and a language barrier had made it difficult to understand her. The guard simply repeated "patients only" as he ushered the young man away from the entrance. Outside, my sister and I stood for a few minutes with others who had been denied entry before we headed back to the car where my husband was waiting.

"Dear God, please help us. We need to be with Mom. All we want is to comfort her." My voice sounded small in the enclosed space. I looked at my sister, her head down in prayer, hands clasped tightly together, reminding me of when we knelt beside our twin beds for nightly prayers in the room we shared as kids. Except this time Mom wasn't with us leading the prayer.

The previous twenty-four hours had been a whirlwind. Yesterday morning we had been on the phone with Mom while she waited for the paramedics to arrive. My brother had special needs. Mom was his caregiver. He was her whole world. The two of them lived together in a two-bedroom condo in Florida. She had gone to wake him up that morning, as was their routine, but found that he had passed away in his sleep. My sister and I stayed on the phone with Mom, trying to calm her, but when the paramedics arrived, they found her in such a state—her heart racing, feeling faint when she tried to stand— they took her to the hospital. She had to leave my brother's body behind, making her even more frantic. Mom called me from the ambulance to let me know what was happening. I reassured her my sister and I would be with her soon.

My sister lives in New Jersey. I live in Texas. We booked the first flights out to Florida, rented a car, and found a hotel room. I recall wondering what was in my suitcase as I boarded the plane. Everything was such a blur that I had no recollection of packing. I just wanted to get to Mom as soon as possible. We arrived that night and were able to speak with Mom on her cell phone. She sounded anxious, but we promised her we would see her in the morning. Now, having just been turned away by the guard, I wasn't sure we would be able to keep that promise.

After our prayer, completely at a loss as to what to do, we sat in silence. I'm not sure how long we sat there before my cell phone rang. The call was from the hospital. A deep voice filled the car. "Hi. My name is David. I'm a nurse and just thought I would reach out with an update on your mom's condition. She is extremely anxious. We've sedated her, but every time she wakes up her heart rate becomes erratic."

I explained to David what I believed to be the reason for Mom's condition. I told him about my brother. How recently he had died. The shock to my mom. How my sister and I had flown in the night before but hadn't been able to see Mom. How our only communication with her had been via her cell phone, and how we had purchased a phone charger for Mom so we could at least keep in touch with her. I spoke fast, trying to relay the urgency. When I finally paused for air, silence filled the car.

Then, David's big, booming voice once more. "This makes a lot more sense to me now. I had no idea she just lost her son. No one mentioned that. Nowhere in her chart does it say that. I'm so sorry for your loss." And, with those words, the floodgates opened. I could no longer hold back the tears.

"Where are you? Can you meet me at the hospital?" We agreed to meet David at the ER entrance. He would make sure Mom got the phone charger.

On the phone David had provided a description of himself, but when we saw him in person it didn't do him justice. His voice matched his stature. He was tall and broad-shouldered, his head shaved bald. He would have looked intimidating if we'd seen him on the street, but we found out that his heart was as big as his presence when he enveloped us in a tight hug. "I'm going to bring one of you in to see your mom. I really think it will help her condition. Your presence will bring her comfort."

In shock, my sister and I debated which one of us would go. Feeling like we were racing against the clock, my sister nudged me toward David and said, "You go. Tell Mom I love her." I looked up at David and he nodded. "Stay right behind me, and don't speak to anyone."

Quickly, I turned back to my sister and hugged her before following David to the ER entrance. As I walked behind him, my heart was racing. I had no idea how we were going to get past the security guard. The hospital doors opened. David stepped inside. I was right behind him. I tried to keep my head down and not look around, but as we approached the guard station, I glanced up. I fully expected to be stopped in our tracks. PATIENTS ONLY. Holding my breath as we walked past the guard, I silently prayed. "Please God, just let me get to Mom." David was moving ahead, so I took a couple of steps to catch up. As I looked back at the guard, we made eye contact, but he didn't make a move.

We turned the corner smack into the middle of a nurse's station. There was uniformed staff everywhere. As I took it all in, I saw a nurse sitting in front of a computer, another hunched over looking at the screen. Three nurses stood at the end of a counter in the middle of a conversation. Nurse's stations are usually a hub of activity, but this one seemed eerily quiet. Once more, I waited for someone to block our approach, call out to David, or question my presence, but every person we passed was frozen. It was as though we were invisible and time was standing still.

We continued past the nurse's station to a row of curtained-off bays. "Please God, let Mom be nearby." Then David pulled back a curtain to reveal a hospital bed where Mom lay. Her face lit up when she saw me.

Every person we passed was frozen. It was as though we were invisible and time was standing still.

I rushed to her side. I hugged and kissed her. I explained that a kind nurse had gotten me in to see her but that it wasn't allowed, and I wasn't sure how long I would be able to stay. I told her my sister was waiting outside. My mom said, "I know which nurse you're talking about. Every time he comes in to see me, he puts his hand on my head, then kisses my forehead before leaving."

Before I could process what Mom had just said, my sister walked in. David had gotten her through as well. My sister and I flanked Mom's bedside. We held hands and prayed. We comforted Mom and let her know that we had made arrangements for my brother's body to be taken care of, and that when she was better we would plan his funeral together. But first she needed to focus on getting strong enough to go home. The last words she said to us as we left were, "Don't worry about me. I'm good. I'm not going to die."

In the days that followed, we weren't able to get in to see her again. It was difficult to get updates without being allowed to enter the hospital. Since we couldn't be with Mom, we focused on sorting through my brother's belongings so she wouldn't have to when she got back home. It was one of the hardest things I'd ever had to do—pack up my deceased brother's items with my heart in a million pieces while also worrying about my mom in the hospital, away from us, with no one to comfort her.

Thirteen days after we saw Mom in the hospital, we got a call from one of the doctors. She had gone into cardiac arrest twice, and twice they had revived her. As he was on the phone with us, she went into cardiac arrest again. He hung up. When he called back later, he told us that Mom had passed. Though the official cause of death was heart failure, I believe that she died of a broken heart.

The days following Mom's passing were filled with sorting and packing up her condo. As my sister and I divided up the sentimental items left behind, we kept replaying those final moments with Mom. The heartbreaking phone call with her while she waited for the paramedics. The desperate prayers in the hospital parking lot. Meeting Nurse David.

Later, my sister shared that the strangest thing had happened when she followed David into the hospital to see Mom. She said it was as though she was invisible to everyone they passed. Like me, she had been terrified that someone would stop them as they made their way through the ER. Instead, it felt like time stood still. Thanks to a stranger who followed his big heart, for one precious hour, as the three of us came together that day, it did.

"You're Alive"

Angela J. Kaufman

You are my hiding place; you will protect me from trouble and surround me with songs of deliverance.
—Psalm 32:7 (NIV)

My feet push the brake pedal as far down as it will go, but I continue to see her bumper fly toward mine. I have done everything in my power to avoid this crash, but in this moment I know it is inevitable.

I'm headed to school on a Saturday afternoon for a solo music contest, because I am the accompanist for many elementary and middle school musicians. Even though it is April and spring has been teasing us, the day is cloudy, and there is a light dusting of snow on the ground. For once, there is not a lot of wind, and the visibility is fine, but the temperature is warm enough to make the fallen snow a muddy mess. I am only three minutes away from the school and left home ahead of schedule. I am driving quite slowly and enjoying the beauty, feeling relaxed despite the stress of performing. In every direction, there is not a single vehicle sharing the road with me. That is, until I see a flash of movement on another street—one that will intersect with mine in about half a block—out of the corner of my eye.

The other car is still a full block from the intersection; I see her blow through a stop sign and barrel toward me. It is obvious that the driver is in a hurry, and I am certain she is not aware of her surroundings. I realize her car will not be able to stop at our intersection due to her speed and the slush on the road. She's heading right for my driver's side door.

You don't have a side airbag.

There's no time to analyze where the inner voice came from or the significance of the phrase. I immediately take evasive action, braking just enough to keep my car from sliding, trying to maneuver myself out of danger. Although the collision is unavoidable, I succeed in shifting to a safer trajectory. Her bumper meets mine with a thud so loud a neighbor comes out to see what has happened.

Her bumper meets mine with a thud so loud a neighbor comes out to see what has happened.

The items in my vehicle slide to the floor. My central nervous system is shaken. I get out of the car to see if she is OK and invite her inside mine so she can get out of the wet snow. She is all decked out, nice hairdo in place, and says she's late going to a party, a wedding shower.

I call in the accident to the local authorities as we wait. I fail to think of taking photos of the car tracks to show she did not brake at all. I let her talk to the officer first once he arrives. As he comes to talk to me, it appears she will be driving away. My brain starts to smoke. *What is going on?*

The officer proceeds to give me a ticket, while I sputter it wasn't my fault, but seem to have no recourse, nor evidence. She was the one who drove through two stop signs, at speeds not conducive to the weather conditions. But I'm too shaken to form the sentence.

As the process winds up, I look at my watch and realize I have time to spare before my next performance. I arrive, collect my thoughts, and calm my nerves. The afternoon finishes on a successful note.

Once home, I relay the events to my husband. This is the first time I have had a chance to look at the ticket I received. I become angry when I see the damage is listed on the wrong side of my car. If the officer had been more careful to mark where I was hit, it would have become apparent that I did not hit her, she hit me.

By now I'm steaming.

Monday morning arrives and I go through the necessary steps to contact my insurance company and get the bumper repaired. Every rehash of the event only adds to my anger.

As I recall what happened later, another detail sticks out: the mysterious voice. *You don't have a side airbag.*

How odd. That is not something I would say or think in that situation. The realization hits me: it was God. A verse from Psalm 91 replays in my mind. "For he will command his angels concerning you to guard you in all your ways; they will lift you up in their hands, so that you will not strike your foot against a stone" (Psalm 91:11–12, NIV). God was telling me a fact, focusing my attention at a critical moment, so I could react in a way that protected both of our lives.

The revelation helps me release some of my anger even as repairs and insurance claims remind me of the accident again. I rehash the trauma of what happened every time I turn the corner at that intersection. Then I hear God's voice once more.

You're alive.

Oh my, how ungrateful I have been. God spared my life, and I am still holding on to bitterness. I sense the need to start practicing the attitude of gratitude every time I drive near the place where the accident happened. From now on, I will acknowledge this incredible act of love and life God has given me.

Instant Comfort

Rhoda Blecker

You will be consoled through them, when you see their ways and their deeds and realize that not without cause did I do all that I did in it—declares the Lord God.
—Ezekiel 14:23 (JPS)

I stood, unhappy and withdrawn, in a corner of the room where the conference welcome reception was taking place. The groups of happy, excited people greeting one another and animatedly talking made me draw back even more into the comparative dimness of my corner. I had been looking forward to this conference for months, but now all I could think was, *Why am I here, instead of at home with Keith?*

Just two days before, my husband, Keith, had been diagnosed with prostate cancer after an anomalous PSA test and the follow-up biopsy. The diagnosis was unexpected; he'd been getting the same anomalous results on his tests for years, but the biopsies had always come back negative. We had just assumed this would be another round of the same process. The diagnosis—and the suspicion that the cancer had been there and been missed in the earlier biopsies—shook us both badly.

I immediately had told Keith I would cancel my attendance at the conference to stay with him. The thought of losing him terrified me, made me want to spend every moment I had with him. But once he was over the initial shock of the diagnosis—he recovered much faster than I did—he argued strenuously with me, and his points were good ones: The meeting was only four days long. The conference was just ninety minutes away this year, and since the organization was international, the next few conferences could be anywhere else in the world, so this was probably my only chance to attend for a long time. I had been burbling about going ever since my registration was confirmed. He had watched me choosing the clothes to take with me, even buying a new shirt (and I had pretty much stopped buying new clothes when I quit working for a corporation and went out on my own).

"This meeting is very special to you," he kept saying.

"So are you!" I told him.

Reasonably—and I have to admit he was always the reasonable one—he said, "I'll be here when you get back. The conference is only here for a short time, and you might never have another chance."

So I let him convince me. I agreed to go as much to make him happy as because I thought the conference might enlighten or entertain me. Leaving him even for such a brief time was frightening.

I have always had a fear of abandonment. My childhood had been a series of relationships developed and lost, some with only a minor impact and some in life-altering ways: When I was only seven, my best friend's family moved away, taking her with them; my parents kept introducing me to kittens or puppies to test whether I was still allergic to them, and took them away again when I started sneezing; my mother died when I was eleven; the first young man I dated seriously was killed in a plane crash just after the relationship started to mean something. It seemed to me that the pattern of my life was loss. And here I was, possibly facing another one.

Standing in the corner of that brightly lit room among happy attendees from all over the world, all I could think was that I was going to lose the husband I loved, and here I was not grabbing every moment I could have with him. What in the world was I doing at this time, in this place?

> *It seemed to me that the pattern of my life was loss. And here I was, possibly facing another one.*

"Are you all right?"

I was startled to hear a quiet question from a woman who had come up to me unnoticed. Ordinarily I would have said I was just fine, even though I must have looked like my picture could illustrate the "misery" entry in the encyclopedia. This time, before I was even aware I was doing it, I told her about Keith's diagnosis and how terrified I was.

She turned back into the room, said, "Wait here," and vanished into the crowd. I thought I must have ruined her experience of the reception, and I felt tears pushing at my eyes. A moment later, however, she was back, accompanied by a smiling man holding a drink. She introduced her husband to me and added, "Let's go to a quieter space."

I let myself be led out of the busy room to some chairs in an out-of-the-way alcove, and the two of them began to tell me their story. It turned out that he had been diagnosed with prostate cancer three years before. They described their reactions, the treatment options available, all the research they had done, how they interviewed different doctors, what their lives were like now—in short, everything I would need to know to handle a process that had seemed overwhelming and unmanageable to me. Most of all, I kept looking at him and thinking, *He went through it, and he's still here. She still has him.*

They gave me their phone numbers and address, along with a list of resources that had been a big help to them. They assured me that, yes, cancer was serious, but it could be gotten through, and they were living proof of that. I couldn't thank them eloquently enough. Though I would never see them again, this seemingly random meeting had made more of a difference than I knew how to express.

As we got up to return to the reception, which was still going strong, he turned back to me and said, "You know, doctors often say that they can *treat* cancer, but when it comes to prostate cancer, you might well hear the doc say that they can *cure* it. Pay attention to that."

It was only after I got back to my hotel room, just before I called Keith, that I realized how much calmer I was. *This* was the unexpected reason I had had to come to the conference—

God had known all along I could find what I needed here. And I understood that the reminder to pay attention really meant more than just listening to the doctors. It also meant listening to God, the ultimate Healer who had Keith and me in His hands.

For Such a Time as This

Kenneth Avon White

Who knows if perhaps you were made queen for just such a time as this?
—Esther 4:14 (NLT)

Everything is bigger in Texas. That's the tagline the state hangs its hat on. The colossal size of Texas may have something to do with the phrase's iconic place in folklore. Once it took me two days just to drive from Houston, my hometown in the southeast, to El Paso at the edge of the western border. Everything is bigger—even the rain.

Closer to the Gulf of Mexico, where I grew up, warm sea air collides with cooler streams from the north to produce Texas-sized rainfalls. Storms could dump water so high and fast that streets with bridge overpasses became our swimming pool. We'd climb up from below and dive right in. It's the same type of rain that came out of nowhere years ago and saved my life, a rain that I came to see as God's hand at work.

At that time, Melanie was my kindergarten sweetheart. It's funny how after almost sixty years I still remember her name. Poignant memories have a way of doing that—creating a homestead in the mind. We both lived in one of the many apartment complexes bumping up against main roads on Houston's south side approaching the even more neglected area of Pasadena. Blue-collar families lived there who couldn't afford to buy a house in the city's more expensive neighborhoods, where tranquil properties ooze comfort and are covered by canopies of mature trees.

The elementary school we attended was less than half a mile away from home. Each school day Melanie and I set out to walk the short distance down the rocky chert road. The day the strange man in a truck picked us up was like any other day. We were about a block from school when he approached. I remember because I could see the flagpole in my school's front yard.

"Hey there," the man yelled out through his opened truck window. "You two want to come see my rabbits? I can write you an excuse for your teacher when I bring you back."

We were beyond excited about the prospect. Moments later, seated in the cab of his truck, we pressed our hands against the dashboard to brace ourselves as the truck made its way to the forest where we were told the rabbits lived.

Not long into the ride, the skies closed in. The sun disappeared. The bottom fell out of the dark clouds above. The stranger became distracted with the relentless downpour. His rabbit stories ceased and instantly he turned from kind to creepy. Melanie began to whimper.

On a dime, the strange man turned back to his kind approach to silence the fuss. I only remember bits and pieces of his stories. There was the mama rabbit—the biggest and fluffiest. Mama rabbit had babies to take care of. The stranger explained to us how that was part of his job—to help the mama rabbit feed her young. We were promised if we were good, we'd be able to feed the rabbits too.

Reaching back into this memory I see the edge of a wide-open field. In the far distance a tall line of trees brings the field to an end. We turned off the main road onto a thin dirt path. A harder, faster rain pounded the truck's hood like a drum. The man raised his voice to be heard over the beat of the raindrops. The bumpy dirt road turned the seat of the cab into a trampoline. Lightning clapped loud, and Melanie again began to whimper. The fun of the moment escaped like air from a deflating balloon.

"How far is it?" I asked.

The truck took its last leap. We landed with a thud. Shrill sounds of the spinning wheels could be heard over the downpour and the thunder.

"My rabbits are in the middle of the woods, so we'll have to walk part of the way," the man said. Sounds of thunder joined the chorus.

Potholes in the sliver of dirt road caused the truck to continue bouncing. Then the truck took its last leap. We landed with a thud. Shrill sounds of the spinning wheels could be heard over the downpour and the thunder. The man pressed on the gas and rocked himself back and forth as if his weight could nudge the truck forward.

He got out of the cab and ordered us to do the same. The back tires were almost entirely buried in a trench carved out in the mud. The stranger slammed his fists on the truck's hood. Looking back, I wonder if this was the moment that he realized his plans had been foiled: he would need help to get out of the mud, and help meant that someone would see him with two obviously frightened children, someone who could identify him—and his truck.

The man ordered us back into the cab, his wet hands slipping up and down our drenched sides as he heaved us up onto the seat. He explained that he needed to go find a wrecker to pull us free. "You stay put till I get back," he barked, and took off across the open field, leaving us alone in the truck. Trained from birth to obey adults unquestioningly, we stayed put. Not long after the stranger left, the rain stopped just as suddenly as it had begun.

It seemed like forever before the man returned with the wrecker and its driver. My memory doesn't tell me whether the driver questioned the situation. I can only imagine the stranger had made up some excuse to explain things away.

Once the truck was free, to our relief, the stranger turned around and drove us back to where he'd picked us up. Two blocks from school, he brought his truck to a halt and scribbled out our notes to explain the tardiness. My memory ends there. I wish I could remember my teacher's reaction. I wish I remembered why I didn't tell Mama that night. If I had told them, I'm sure there would have been fallout. I would remember that.

But I am convinced of one thing: had Melanie and I walked into the woods that day, we would have never walked out.

God sent the rain to stop the truck, and He saved my life and Melanie's.

And since that day, my life has been shaped by knowing this: Wherever I am headed, God is in my future before I ever get there. God is always working things out for my good. This has helped me renew my mind with right thinking, which affects how I respond both to the good and the not so good. I ask far less "why, Lord?" and spend more time in prayer asking for clarity: "How do you want me to respond and when?" For me, this line of reverent questioning opens up a whole new channel of communicating with God. His answers resonate with my healed soul and empower me to live out a purpose-driven life.

It's a similar path I see the Bible's Queen Esther walking. Everything she went through on her way to the throne helped fulfill the greater purpose of saving her people from Haman's decree of death. For me, going through this experience has given me a sense of justice and purpose—a drive to stand up for and protect the innocent in both group and individual settings, and to be cautious around people who might not be what they seem.

I am convinced that everything God has brought me through is no coincidence, including my second chance at life. Like Esther, He has been preparing me "for such a time as this."

GOD'S MYSTERIOUS WAYS: THE RIGHT TIME

In the book of Esther, a young Jewish girl is taken to be a concubine to King Xerxes, and her beauty is so great that he makes her his queen. But when a member of the court plots to enslave and kill the Jews, her foster father Mordecai urges her to intervene in a line that modern readers often find themselves relating to: "And who knows but that you have come to your [current] position for such a time as this?"

Do you believe that God has a reason for everything that happens, even the tragedies? That anything can be turned around to a positive end if we allow it to be? Here are some ways to explore that idea:

- **Pray.** Talk to God about a time when you were hurt, or a time when you saw others suffering. Be open to His answers about why it happened.

- **Seek.** Keeping that same situation in mind, consider: Are there ways that good can come out of it? Are you in a place right now where you can do something to make a difference?

- **Act.** Sometimes sharing about a difficult experience, or acting to support people who are suffering, can encourage others to do the same. Is there anything that you can do today to use past hurts to help others?

- **Reflect.** Why do you think God has put you in the place where you are?

Pointing Me in the Right Direction

Diane Stark

*In your unfailing love you will lead
the people you have redeemed.*
—Exodus 15:13 (NIV)

I had a job interview in an hour, and my car wouldn't start. I ran back into the house and asked my stepdad, Doug, if he could take a look at my car.

Immediately, he tossed me his car keys. "Today is too important. Take my car and we'll worry about fixing yours later."

"But your car is brand-new. You've had it less than a week."

He waved his hand through the air. "It's just a car. This job interview could impact your whole future. Yours and the kids."

I gave him a quick hug and ran out the door. I climbed into his just-off-the-lot SUV and carefully backed down the driveway. I appreciated that Doug loaned me his car, but driving it just added to my nervousness.

Doug was right. A lot was riding on this interview. I had to land the job. I was going through a divorce, and my two young kids and I had recently moved across the state to stay with my parents for a few months. Before separating from my husband, I'd taught preschool kids with special needs. I'd loved it, but I had to resign when we moved. Now I needed to find a new teaching position. After sending out dozens of résumés, I'd only been offered one interview—at a middle school nearly an hour from our house. I'd never taught middle school. In fact, I joked that I had a rule against teaching kids who were taller than I am, and I'm only five feet tall. Plus, the lengthy commute would be tough on my already-broken-down car and leave my kids in day care far longer than I wanted. It wasn't my dream job, but school was starting the following week. This position was my only option.

I needed this job, even if I didn't really want it.

I was about halfway there when something on the dashboard caught my eye. One of those "idiot lights" had come on. "How could this happen?" I muttered. "It's a brand-new car."

Something on the dashboard caught my eye. One of those "idiot lights" had come on. "How could this happen?" I muttered. "It's a brand-new car."

I pulled into a gas station to figure out what to do. I was digging through the glove box to find the owner's manual when a man tapped on the window and asked if I needed help.

"The light that looks like an exclamation point just came on, and I don't know what it means," I said.

"It's the low tire pressure warning," he said. "There's an air compressor over there."

I thanked him and drove across the parking lot, wondering how I'd figure out which tire was low.

I was digging through my purse for coins to pay for the air when the man walked over, carrying a pressure gauge. "I'd be glad to take care of this. I don't want you to get your clothes dirty," he said, nodding toward my blouse and skirt.

"I really appreciate that. I'm on my way to a job interview, and I don't want to show up late—or dirty."

He bent down to check a tire and asked where I was interviewing.

"I'm a teacher. My interview is at a middle school about thirty minutes from here."

"That's funny. I just got an email from my kids' school this morning. They need to hire another kindergarten teacher, and since school is starting so soon, they asked us parents to refer any qualified candidates we know directly to the principal."

Kindergartners were sure to be shorter than me. "Where's the school?" I asked. My mouth dropped open when he told me. "You're not going to believe this, but I attended that school when I was a kid. It's right around the corner from my house. I would love to teach there."

"You should apply," he said.

My shoulders slumped. "I already did. I sent my résumé to the school district's main office two months ago. I never heard back."

"This job was just added. Enrollment was larger than expected, so they need another kindergarten teacher. This position didn't even exist until yesterday. You need to call the principal right away and request an interview."

"I'll do that. Thank you."

The man stood up from checking the last tire. "None of your tires are low. I don't know why the light came on, but you should be good to get to your interview."

I smiled and thanked him for his help. As I headed to the interview at the middle school, I called the principal about the kindergarten position. She agreed to meet with me the following morning.

When she offered me the job on the spot, I knew exactly why the tire pressure light on Doug's brand-new SUV had come on, despite all the tires being inflated to the right level. God used that exclamation point light to point me in the right direction—and right to my perfect new job.

The Wind

Lowell Bartel

When the day of Pentecost came, they were all together in one place. Suddenly a sound like the blowing of a violent wind came from heaven and filled the whole house where they were sitting. They saw what seemed to be tongues of fire that separated and came to rest on each of them. All of them were filled with the Holy Spirit and began to speak in other tongues as the Spirit enabled them.

—Acts 2:1–4 (NIV)

I've read the Pentecost story in Acts countless times, always attracted to the mystery. But I never expected to experience it myself.

Jews from all over the world travel to Jerusalem for Shavuot, the annual Feast of Pentecost. Two thousand years ago, those pilgrims included the twelve disciples of Jesus. Suddenly a strong wind blew through their house, igniting a verbal wildfire that touched each one of them. The disciples began to speak at once, praising God in a tangle of tongues. The great loud wind drew a crowd of other Jews who gathered outside their house. Everyone heard the disciples praising

God in their own native language! Christians call that wind the Holy Spirit.

As senior pastor of Milwaukee's Bay View Methodist Church, I attended the annual conference of Methodist churches in Wisconsin. One year we learned that Milwaukee was launching a Hispanic Methodist church; the founding pastor, Luis Gonzales, stood to be recognized.

During our next break, I made my way through the chairs, keeping my eye on Luis. Luis enthusiastically shook my hand, brown eyes crinkling, smile wide. As we talked about plans for the new church, he explained in lightly accented English, "We will worship in a storefront, but are still looking for some office space."

"We can get you some space in our church," I offered.

My congregation followed up on my promise by equipping the room with a typewriter, telephone, desk, and chair. It was a pleasure for me to stop by Luis's office often to ask, "How's it going?" and to sit down to hear his full reply.

As our friendship grew, we often attended events at each other's churches. At first, to augment their handful of Hispanic worshipers, groups from my church would join Luis's congregation for services. Since the visitors spoke only English, and most of his congregation spoke only Spanish, Luis alternated languages as he preached. When I preached there, either Pastor Luis or Gus, a lay Hispanic leader I knew well, translated for me. The Methodist hymns and the Lord's Prayer were even more joyful when lifted together in both languages. As new immigrants moved in, our two congregations worked together to meet their needs, everything from housing and household goods to jobs and English classes.

When the Hispanic congregation outgrew their storefront, they searched for a suitable building to purchase, assisted by an architect from our Bay View congregation. Everyone applauded the day Luis moved his office into their new church. I shook his hand. "I'm happy for you, my friend. But I'm sorry I won't see you as often." We pledged to stay in touch.

Several months later, Luis called to ask if I could preach on a Sunday when he'd be away. I responded, "As long as Gus is available to translate, I would consider it an honor."

As I stood before the congregation to lead worship, each child, youth, and adult smiled warmly at me, and I at them. Gus introduced my sermon: *"Hoy día nuestro amigo Lowell nos traerá el mensaje."* ("Today our friend Lowell will bring us the message.")

Gus and I faced the congregation, side by side. I spoke two or three sentences in English, then Gus repeated them in Spanish. We continued that rhythm for several minutes.

At my next pause, Gus turned to face me. Softly but earnestly, he said, "Lowell, you don't need me anymore."

Startled out of the flow of my sermon, I blinked. "You gotta be kidding me!"

Gus smiled, "No, I'm not kidding. You don't need me. They understand you."

I tipped my head to one side, frowning in confusion. On my friend's face I saw peace and acceptance. And something else: trust. "OK, Gus. I believe you." Gus sat down.

I took a long, slow breath. I resumed my sermon in English.

What happened next felt like a waking dream. The listeners were with me, I was with them, and the outside world was irrelevant.

Although I was the only one speaking out loud, it proceeded like a dialogue. The congregation responded to my words with nods or "Amen" in the right places. I spoke in English and they heard in Spanish. Or perhaps they heard with a deeper part of themselves.

After the service, I greeted the congregation. I grasped their hands tightly with both of mine, and saw in their shining eyes the same love that filled me. We exchanged enthusiastic smiles and shared a connection that went beyond words.

Together we had glimpsed the mystery, the spirit, of God. Living, breathing, powerful, impossible to capture. Like the wind.

A Sister-in-Christ from God

Nyla Kay Wilkerson

For where two or three gather in my name, there am I with them.

—Matthew 18:20 (NIV)

My husband, Dennis, had been sick for a long time, longer than even I realized. Oh, I knew he wasn't acting like himself, but he kept insisting that everything was fine. One morning, at a time when he should have been at his office leading an important meeting, I found him sitting in his favorite chair in our garage. That was when we both knew that something was very wrong.

After many doctor visits, tests, and prescriptions, it was determined that Dennis suffered from hypoparathyroidism. This is a condition which causes mood swings, irritability, depression, muscle cramps, and a litany of other symptoms. On top of that, he had advanced COPD, chronic obstructive pulmonary disease.

Our lives changed drastically. Dennis became a recluse. He refused to leave the house and would only see our children and my parents. Friends quit calling and stopping in to visit.

He wanted me by his side 24/7. Fortunately I worked from home and could accommodate him. As he got sicker, he did not even want me to talk on the phone or leave the house.

Family and friends did not understand why I stopped attending social functions and family gatherings. It did not matter that the doctors had placed an expected deadline on my husband's life. Some were so callous as to suggest that I divorce or at least separate from him. My wedding vows said "in sickness and in health," so I would not even consider either one.

I have a passion for reading Christian books of all types, and reading is something that I could do and still be close to my husband, so I joined a reviewers' club organized by a woman named Kari. Once a month we met online.

One afternoon as I was praying, God said to me, *You are going to win a door prize tonight. When Kari calls you, ask her to pray for Dennis.* I was stunned, but I knew if God said it, it was going to happen.

When the meeting went into a break so that Kari could phone the door-prize winner, I patiently waited for the phone to ring. Sure enough, it did. I answered it by saying, "Hello, Kari, I knew you were going to call me." She laughed and asked me how, thinking it was because of the power of caller ID. After I told her it was because God told me she was going to call, and He had instructed me to request that she pray for Dennis, all laughter ceased.

"Why does your husband need prayer?" she asked.

As I explained his health issues, she immediately understood exactly how I felt. She had walked this road before me; her husband had the same parathyroid condition, and her family and friends hadn't understood when his behavior changed. Before we ended our call, she insisted on praying for my husband and me. It was a Spirit-filled prayer that started a lifelong friendship between us.

Later, I would learn that the first person whose name was chosen had a disconnected telephone number. The second person did not answer their phone. So Kari asked her daughter to go through the list of names and randomly choose one. Her daughter immediately settled on mine because it rhymed with hers—one of a series of seeming coincidences that showed us God had been guiding us toward this meeting.

Before we ended our call, she insisted on praying for my husband and me. It was a Spirit-filled prayer that started a lifelong friendship between us.

After that initial telephone call, we emailed back and forth, and learned we had a plethora of things in common. Our love and service to God was the main one. We adored our husbands and children, read an exorbitant number of Christian books, and had many favorite things in common, including coffee. Her daughter and I both had unusual names, and we each received our names at the last minute after others had already been chosen.

Soon we progressed from emails to phone calls. Each phone call began with a prayer. We became prayer partners and sisters in Christ so naturally. Even though there was a fifteen-year difference in our ages and four hundred miles separating our homes, we became best friends.

What one person needed, the other provided. We learned to put God first and start our phone calls with prayer. Praising, interceding, thanking, and humbly asking God things in prayer was a daily habit. Always we asked Him to let us be a blessing to someone. When we chatted, we talked about what was happening in our lives and God.

We each had a sister, but this sisterhood in Christ was totally different. Our boundaries were there were no boundaries. Complete honesty was a requirement. When one of us struggled, the other one was there to offer assistance, support, and cheer. Five years after we met, Kari helped me through one of the toughest years of my life when my family was struck by a series of deaths: my husband, my dad, my grandson, my aunt, and my fifteen-year-old dog. She spent many hours praying for me, which strengthened me during those dark days. I reciprocated when she had family issues.

On that book club meeting evening, it was no coincidence that the first two phone calls did not connect. Nor is it a coincidence that Kari's daughter's name rhymes with mine, causing her to pick my name as the winner. How about Kari's husband having the same parathyroid issue or her friends and family responding in the same way mine did? No, these were not coincidences at all. These were God-incidences, which are the perfect kind. God knew exactly what I needed and when. He orchestrated the phone call that gave me the beautiful sister-in-Christ that I was missing.

A Voice from the Flames

Ellen Akemi Crosby

But Jeremiah said, "They will not turn you over. Please obey the Lord *in what I am saying to you, that it may go well with you and you may live."*

—Jeremiah 38:20 (NASB)

It was another summer's day. Sacramento's sweltering weather made mirages of solid objects. I got out of bed to face the long commute from my home in Fair Oaks, California, to *The Sacramento Bee*, the area's largest daily metropolitan newspaper. Most conversations at *The Bee* centered on the drought that was currently affecting the state—would it continue much longer? Bets were made on how high temperatures would reach that day, praises were sent up to the inventor of air conditioning, and everyone dreaded getting into their car after it had baked all day in the sun.

Breaking news about the forest fires in the Sierra Nevada foothills flooded the media. The danger was extremely high, but far away—or so I thought. The call from my husband, Paul, came in the afternoon. His voice was tense. He measured his words carefully.

"You'd better come home; our house is on fire!"

My mind whirled. My only clear thought was for the safety of my husband and my precious four-year-old daughter. Paul was all right, and, with reassurances from him that Justine was safe, I bolted out of my chair and rushed directly to my boss's office. "My house is on fire; I need to go home!" It was not a request, it was a statement of fact.

Speeding down Interstate 80, I remember saying out loud over and over, "Oh, dear Lord, please get me there in one piece so I can help my family!"

Then I saw it. Our home, our personal sanctuary, had almost completely burned to the ground.

I had so many thoughts and fears rushing through my mind. God must have sent angels to guide the car, because I remember little of how I got to my neighborhood. There were so many cars it looked like the parking lot when the state fair is in full swing. Desperately, I forced my car into a space several blocks away and sprinted clumsily in my high heels.

Frantically weaving and shoving my way through the crowd, I saw that my block was cordoned off like a crime scene. Undeterred, I ducked under the tape and kept going.

A fireman put his hand on my shoulder. "No one is allowed past this point!"

I glared at him. "See that house right there with all the smoke? That's mine!"

His eyes softened, he loosened his grip, and waved me through.

Several fire trucks battled the fire, which had engulfed three duplexes, leaving six families homeless. The air was filled with smoke and an acrid smell, a mixture of wood, metal, and plastic. Because the entrance to my street was impassable, I was forced to take the street behind my house all the way to the end of the block and then double back to reach my home. I was astonished to see people watching from their lawn chairs with ice chests of drink and food.

How dare they! This isn't an outdoor concert! I fumed inwardly. I felt like upending their ice chests and dumping their contents all over the sidewalk. But my family was more important. I hurried on.

Nearing my home, I found my husband, his parents, and other members of the family standing on the sidewalk across the street from our house. I scanned the area for Justine. "Where is she? Is she hurt?" I gasped, then breathed easier when I saw her in our pickup truck across the street.

Then I saw it. Our home, our personal sanctuary, had almost completely burned to the ground. The garage was still intact, but I could see all the way to the back wall where my bedroom was a smoke-stained, waterlogged mess. Gone were my daughter's room, the dining room, and the living room. Denial and disbelief set in immediately. Shock, anger, and hurt would follow soon after.

That evening, we gathered at my in-laws' house, and Paul told us the astounding story of how he and Justine had escaped the fire.

Paul had been awake, but resting in the bedroom since his job required him to get up in the early morning hours. Justine was watching *The Flintstones* on TV. Suddenly, she heard a voice urge her to go to the sliding glass door and look out.

She looked around and called, "Daddy?"

No response. She went back to watching Fred and Barney speed-pedal their car to work.

The voice, a little louder this time, entreated again. This time, unafraid, she quickly obeyed.

She reached the door and pushed aside the drapes to peer out. Wide-eyed, she saw reddish-orange flames just feet away. Twenty feet away, across a short fence, our landlord's house was engulfed in flame. The fire had jumped from our landlord's roof to ours.

Justine rushed to the bedroom crying, "Daddy, daddy!"

Paul leapt off the bed, thinking Justine was hurt.

"Fred's house is on fire!" she called. Fred was our landlord's name.

Seeing the same frightful scene, he knew he had minutes, maybe seconds to get them both out. He snatched up his composed, but bewildered, daughter and flew out the front door. He gently placed her out of harm's way and rushed back inside to retrieve anything worth saving. He grabbed his treasured Guild guitar and some cash. Bolting out of our smoke-filled home, he heard windows exploding, glass shattering from the intense heat. There was no going back.

Later, a police report and news coverage filled in the blanks on what had happened. A disgruntled former tenant decided to exact undeserved revenge on our landlords by setting their redwood deck on fire. The heat and winds fed the fire and it spread.

That night as we settled in to sleep in my in-laws' house, I said a prayer of thanksgiving to the Lord for protecting my loved ones. In the closet hung the dress I had worn that day, with my matching pumps set right below it on the floor. A stray moonbeam found its way through the curtains, a single spotlight illuminating my dress. It was a reminder to me that the material things in life were only temporary pleasures; what really counted were the people who I loved and who loved me. It is my underlying faith in God and that of my family that keep me strong and ready for life's challenges.

That faith would be tested. The next morning, as we rummaged through what once was our home, I was struck by how utterly complete the damage was. There was really nothing left; no discernable shapes or colors could be seen. If a life were measured by material things, then it was as if my family and I never existed.

As I moved toward the back part of the house, I made a discovery that would always stand out in my memories of the fire. What was once Justine's bedroom was merely a gray-black carpet of ash. The lone survivor in my little girl's room was the crisp, rusted-looking box springs of her first "big girl" bed. I bent down slowly to touch them. Gratitude flooded my heart that Justine was alive and would sleep in another big-girl bed again someday—my young daughter who had heard the Lord's voice and obeyed.

But there was another find that became the most remarkable legacy of the fire, standing as a testament to my God's enduring faithfulness and my family's resilience. Among the soot-covered remains of my husband's belongings was his well-loved, oft-read Bible. Just as Meshach, Shadrach, and Abednego withstood Nebuchadnezzar's furnace in the book of Daniel, this book of the Word of God withstood the inferno in our home. Paul would, in the aftermath, gently and precisely separate the singed pages and apply duct tape to temporarily repair the cover and binding. Later, he would have this life-changing book professionally rebound—reborn and risen from the ashes. When he brought it home, I couldn't help but draw parallels to our Savior's death and resurrection as I brushed my fingers gently across its new cover.

The Power of Secret Giving

Diane Buller

But when you give to the needy, do not let your left hand know what your right hand is doing, so that your giving may be in secret. Then your Father, who sees what is done in secret, will reward you.

—Matthew 6:3–4 (NIV)

"Tell me who they're from!" I pleaded, cradling a dozen perfectly arranged red roses in my arms. The deliveryman shrugged and pointed to the card. It read, "A Secret Admirer."

Just a week before, a two-year relationship I'd been in had ended, leaving me broken and dreading my thirtieth birthday. All that week I struggled to teach Edgar Lee Masters's *Spoon River Anthology* to my high-school American Literature classes. Usually, the collection was one of my top-five favorites to teach. But, consumed with self-doubt and wallowing in regret, I snipped at a student who didn't have his book again. My hopes and dreams had been crushed with another failed relationship. Surely my life was headed in reverse! I just wanted to hide, or at least make it to lunchtime without breaking down in a puddle of tears.

Every school day, at least a half dozen of us gathered with Tupperware or the occasional cafeteria tray to share lunch in the Home Economics room. Mostly, we women laughed, whined, bantered, and shared stories for nearly thirty minutes, bell-to-bell. A much-valued reprieve. *Is the pain written all over my face?* I vowed not to tell anyone my story. I tried to carry on with my life as if nothing had happened.

Never one to appreciate a secret or surprise, I pondered the extravagant gift of roses with no signature. *Who gives a gift and doesn't sign their name, anyway? Why?* I did know I liked the word the sender had used: Admire.

After a couple awkward phone calls, I gave up trying to find the mysterious sender. Until the next afternoon. After teaching all day at school, I rushed into the local florist. Finding one of my high school students working there, I begged him to tell me who sent the roses. Reluctantly, he revealed the name.

Sooner rather than later, the life I had sought found me. An old acquaintance reconnected and romance bloomed. Between the flurry of marriage, moves, babies, and classes, and the practical fact of no longer living in the same city, I forgot about my secret admirer.

Ten-plus years later, a funeral visitation out of town brought a couple of us teacher friends together. How much I had missed them! Reminiscing and reflecting after the visitation spurred me to action. I penned a long overdue thank-you letter to my secret admirer: an older teacher who taught business classes in another wing. She had somehow learned of my breakup saga and sent those roses, anonymously, to lift my spirits.

I had never asked her how she'd discovered my situation. Except for those lunches, we seldom encountered each other. Her hard stories of growing up in North Carolina and working in the tobacco fields could stop a conversation. An overcomer, she was bold and a bit blunt. Brimming with faith. Everything I longed for. And *admired!* With three children of her own, I feel sure that she didn't have an abundance of cash even though she gifted me such an extravagant gift on that damp March morning.

Now, reminded of the kindness I'd received, I realized that I could do more than just express gratitude—I could follow her example.

With the holiday decorations starting to pop up, I knew where to start. A young father at church had abruptly lost his job. Familiar with the backstory, I felt confident the need was significant for the family of five. Instead of the usual "I should," this time I acted on the need. Parking my minivan down the street at dusk, I prayed, then dropped off a gift bag with a game and new books for the children. I added a gift card and signed the greeting card that I placed in the bag, "Friends." I rang the doorbell and ran. I was still smiling when I went home to start dinner.

When our son went through a difficult situation at school, I thought of the coach who had encouraged him. I waited until the end of the season, then mailed a gift card and note to him at school. "Thank you for coaching our son." More recently, a single mom I met through a mentoring group needed the reminder, "You're an unsung hero!" A doorstep drop-off that time. I asked Gary to sign the card so she wouldn't recognize my writing. A team effort.

And there was the unimaginable. A woman and her children were spending the night at a hotel to avoid her abusive husband. Her daughter and mine were friends. A phone call to the front desk took care of their night.

It's prayer that directs my *if, when,* and *where* to give. It's all God's idea anyway. Maybe it is just a little bit of "love" dropped on the front porch or a gift card inside a greeting card. Or a little more. God has always provided me with enough.

Have any lives been changed with my secret gifting? I don't know. I do know that mine has, both then and still today. And I never would have had the push to get started if it hadn't been for that long-ago bouquet of roses.

A few days after I mailed the thank-you letter, I got a call from my secret admirer. "Your letter made me cry," she said. Those roses had changed my life! They graced my desk and heart when I desperately needed them. Her single act of anonymous giving showed me the power of an act of loving kindness that shows up out of nowhere at the perfect time.

My first sight of that beautiful bouquet is still freeze-framed in my mind. A catalyst of hope, it helped reroute me. What an important marker in my timeline! To gift someone hope needs a prayer—but not always a signature.

GOD'S MYSTERIOUS WAYS: GOD-GIVEN FRIENDS

One of God's favorite ways to intervene in our lives is to send people across our path who can help us, or whom we can help. Sometimes those encounters are brief—we have stories in this volume of people who were helped by a stranger or strangers who they never saw again, for example—but sometimes those chance encounters lead to lifelong friendships.

Do you have a God-given friend or friends? Are you wishing for one? Here are some steps you can take to be more open to the possibilities:

- **Pray.** Take a moment in your prayer time to thank God for the friends in your life who have made a difference, or your hopes if you're hoping for new ones.

- **Seek.** Be open when you meet new people. Not everyone you meet has the potential to become a good friend, but taking an extra moment to talk might reveal a connection you didn't know existed.

- **Act.** Tell a friend how much they mean to you, or how much you appreciate the things that they do.

- **Reflect.** Looking back on past friendships, can you see God's hand bringing you together?

The Eleventh Hour

A. J. Larry

You can be sure that God will take care of everything you need, his generosity exceeding even yours in the glory that pours from Jesus.
—PHILIPPIANS 4:19 (MSG)

We'd heard it said that God sometimes comes at the eleventh hour, and my husband, John, and I believed it, having seen a lifetime of God's on-time blessings. Even our hardships—whether we brought them upon ourselves or not—have proven to be blessings in disguise. But never had we imagined that God's blessings would appear in such an amazing way as they did on that final day that the bank was due to seize our business property.

After fourteen years of operating a childcare business—a business that blossomed from five students to a bustling capacity of 109 students—we'd been forced to close our doors. We'd lost our financial footing. Amid the economic downturn of 2007, we became more unstable as most of our private clients, who made up nearly half of our childcare enrollment, inopportunely lost their jobs. We bemoaned their losses. We mourned the loss of our faithful and hardworking employees, who we were forced to lay off because of low enrollment.

But mostly, we regretted the loss to our daughters, who had invested their blood, sweat, and tears into making our family business succeed.

As enrollments dwindled and we understood that we would not be able to continue, we obtained a real estate agent to help us decide on a selling price for the building. But after a few months and no buyer prospects, we had to reduce the price we'd settled on. Our plans to sell the property, pay off the existing mortgage, and clear other looming debts were beginning to look hopeless. Worse, we had been so struck by remorse that we had neglected to organize a projected sale of indoor and outdoor furnishings. As the deadline loomed, it was too late to analyze and take inventory of the mountain of wee tables and chairs, wall art, infant beds, and office furniture. Too late to place items on eBay; too late to consider an auction or a going-out-of-business sale. And since no solid buyer prospects had surfaced, we stood the chance of losing it all.

Too quickly, it was the last day. We had until five o'clock to pay off our debts before the bank took possession of our property. John and I drove in silence to our childcare facility for our final chance to pick up any keepsakes. Our resolve was to focus on God rather than our circumstances. As we exited the car, I glanced at John and noticed his jaw muscle tighten, as if preparing himself to brave the great emotional tension of our last visit to our facility. We entered at the side door. When we reached the main hallway, we walked our separate ways.

I trudged from one room to the next, weighing up the memories against the losses. The sweat equity our family had wrought together, instructing, teaching, counseling, praying with our students and their families. The stamp of approval was the students' artwork that lined the walls. I passed the toddler room and paused at the door of the infant room. So many times I'd left my office and made my way there to seek refuge among the soft cries and coos of the infants, regaining my calm on a hectic day.

I found John sometime later in the spacious front classroom that we had tagged the "blue room" because of its expansive blue carpet. We came together at the "reading bench," an old church pew that had been refurbished and installed against a long wall under a high window. We began reminiscing and thanking God for the people who'd changed us and the lives we'd changed. We sang praises to our God and exchanged our favorite childcare stories and laughed until we cried.

We had until five o'clock to pay off our debts before the bank took possession of our property.

In the midst of our tears of joy, a car pulled up. A man and two women stepped out of the car and came up to the door of our facility. As John welcomed them in, the unsmiling but not ungentle-faced man asked if they could have a walk-through of the facility. We happily obliged.

As they perused the facility, John and I noticed the fixed regard on the gentleman's face. His purposeful steps as he strode from classroom to classroom. His close attention to detail as he scanned the ceilings and floors of the facility. As we concluded the walk-through, the man, seemingly pleased, told us that he was interested in the property and wanted to draw up a contract. "Today," he said. He wanted a two-year, triple net lease, with the option to buy in "as is" condition, including all indoor and outdoor furnishings.

John and I exchanged glances, both of us astonished by the visitors' sudden appearance, sense of mission, and the all-inclusiveness of the offer. We would never know how God brought our facility to his attention; we assumed that he had been eyeing the property, realizing from the low activity that there might be an opportunity for him to buy. But on that very day? The man didn't seem to be aware of our impending five o'clock deadline. God had brought us the buyer we needed, and we knew we had to trust Him to complete what had been started.

After negotiating for a short while longer, the man and John headed to a real estate broker's office to draw up a contract. John came rushing back to the center with an official check in hand representing the deposit for the property—an amount large enough to satisfy our debts with the bank.

It was close to four o'clock when we arrived at the bank to deposit the official check. As we made our way into the bank, we anxiously waited in line for assistance and watched as time slipped swiftly away from us. When we finally stood before the bank representative to make our deposit, it was almost five o'clock—the eleventh hour!

Storm Shelter

Nancy Shelton, as told to Marci Seither

But God made the earth by his power; he founded the world by his wisdom and stretched out the heavens by his understanding. When he thunders, the waters in the heavens roar; he makes clouds rise from the ends of the earth. He sends lightning with the rain and brings out the wind from his storehouses.

—Jeremiah 10:12–13 (NIV)

Being stranded without a way home and having a car stuck in the mud were two things I never really cared for, and being stranded *because* I was stuck was even less appealing to me. Throw in a long dirt road, an oncoming cloudburst, and a tank crossing, and that pretty much summed up the night I prayed for a miracle.

My boyfriend, Todd, and I had married right after I graduated from college. As newlyweds we moved to an Army base in Korea, and then a few years later Todd was stationed at Fort Polk, Louisiana. We lived at the edge of the large post in base housing.

Since we hadn't yet started a family, I decided I should take the time to go back to college—a sixty-mile drive each way.

Driving on the flat terrain wasn't an issue for me, but the roads got very slippery when it rained. The thick dust would turn to a sludge that you could easily sink into if you were not careful. I knew from a previous incident—where just a tap of the brakes during a light rain had sent me into a tailspin—that you could lose control in the blink of an eye.

The road from the base to school was a long stretch, and at the time it was under construction. It had surprised me, the first time I'd driven that way, to see the "tank crossing" sign at what felt like the middle of nowhere. No doubt the heavy treads running over asphalt were part of the reason the road was in need of repair.

That day I got out of my advanced math class and headed for home. Approaching the construction zone, I could see dark clouds ahead. Even though it was only a five-mile stretch of road being worked on, the asphalt had been removed, leaving nothing but dirt, and it slowed traffic down so much it took at least thirty minutes to travel the section.

A gentle rain would actually keep the dust down—but you just didn't want to be on that kind of road in the middle of nowhere when it started to rain. And the clouds on the horizon were not like the rain clouds that drifted along in a children's picture book. They were boiling masses of dark grays that tumbled against each other like pounding surf, accentuated with bolts of lightning crashing across the sky. These were the kinds of clouds that dropped buckets of rain, turning a dusty road to a miry bog within minutes. The tank crossing was ahead, and I worried that it might not be easy for someone in a tank to spot the little blue Toyota Corolla I was driving if I slid off the road, since there wasn't a shoulder to pull off on.

"Please hold the rain!" I asked the Lord, remembering the Bible stories where the Lord kept it from raining until the perfect time. "If You could hold off the rain until the animals were in the ark with Noah, or calm the storm when the disciples were afraid, could You please take notice of a Midwest girl who just wants to get home safely?"

"Please hold the rain!" I asked the Lord, remembering the Bible stories where the Lord kept it from raining until the perfect time.

I could feel my grip tightening on the steering wheel. I kept my eyes on the road, glancing to my right and left for any sign of tanks out on maneuvers. My stomach tightened as I braced for what I feared was coming, being stranded and stuck in the mud. It was before cell phones, and I knew if I got stuck it could be hours before another car passed. I had no way to get ahold of Todd to let him know where I was.

"Please, just hold the rain," I prayed fervently. The clouds got closer.

The haze underneath the clouds told me that they were moving much faster than I was moving. Rain. And a lot of it. Dark and eerie.

The dust continued to billow from under my tires. I couldn't go any faster without losing control, so I just kept praying.

The edge of the dirt construction zone was in sight. The pavement kept getting closer, but so did the storm clouds.

It was going to be close. I kept praying. As soon as my tires rolled from the dirt to the smooth surface of the asphalt, the rain began to fall in sheets. The timing was perfect. God's timing is always perfect.

I had prayed many times in my life, but that day I felt especially vulnerable. The whole way home I sang hymns that I had played in church for years. "What Can Wash Away My Sins" was at the top of my list.

God has been in the washing business since He created the earth, but now more than ever I trusted that He was just as faithful in the waiting business as well. If He could create the clouds and rain, He could slow the storm enough for me to get home safe.

God's Divine Delay

Nicole N. Brown

For my own name's sake I delay my wrath; for the sake of my praise, I hold it back from you, so as not to destroy you completely. See, I have refined you, though not as silver; I have tested you in the furnace of affliction.

—Isaiah 48:9–10 (NIV)

It's often said that delay is not denial. That is comforting. However, to me, it's more comforting to know that with God, delay is often divine.

It was my final semester of a long college journey, one that had me take on a grueling schedule of going to school full time, working part time, and interning at my favorite radio station, where I had my sights set on future employment. Through it all, my focus was sharper than ever. I had solicited help for certain subjects when I needed it, and I was in the home stretch, excited and pumped to reach the finish line.

This morning, however, I was running late for class. For reasons I didn't fully understand at the time, I was procrastinating. Taking my time. Finding everything to do other than leave for school.

I decided to curl my hair. As I was doing my hair in the bathroom, I heard a crackling sound coming from my mother's bedroom. At first, I was hesitant to go into her room because she was sound asleep, and I didn't want to wake her. However, I felt a persistent nudge, which I now know was the Holy Spirit. The incessant nudge got stronger and stronger until I obeyed.

As I slowly walked towards her room, I began focusing my ears, still trying to distinguish this unfamiliar sound and where it was coming from. When I entered the room, the desire to identify the cause became more intense. As I walked around to my mother's bedside, I noticed against the wall, on the carpeted floor next to curtains, there was a candle in a glass jar. It was lit, and it looked as if it had been burning all night. There was only an inch of wax left to burn before it would connect to the carpet and start an uncontrollable fire.

Immediately, I rushed over to extinguish the fire and pick up the jar, but the glass was so hot that I couldn't touch it with my bare hands. I ran back to the bathroom to turn off my curling iron and get a cloth that I could use to remove the candle with care. Throughout it all, my mother slept soundly. She had been prescribed sleep medication for a medical condition, and she might not have been woken even by the sound or heat of a fire in the house.

Thankfully, I was able to remove the candle without getting burned or dropping it. I quickly got it to the bathroom and extinguished it.

God, in His sovereignty, grace, and loving kindness, divinely delayed me from leaving the house sooner. Only He knows what would have happened if I hadn't been procrastinating, if I hadn't been struck by the strange urge to stop and curl my hair when I was already running late, if I hadn't happened to hear the sound of the candle.

As I look back over that day, the days surrounding that time, and other periods of my life, I can clearly see God's providence through it all. There have been so many revealing moments of His hand in my life. That day will forever leave an indelible mark of His love for me and my mom. I'm grateful for God's divine delay.

Thankful for Stomach Pain

Melissa Henderson

Consider it pure joy, my brothers and sisters, whenever you face trials of many kinds, because you know that the testing of your faith produces perseverance.

—James 1:2–3 (NIV)

Piercing stabs of pain in my abdomen had increased over three days. What started as a slight ache had turned to severe agony. Cradling my stomach, I wondered about the cause.

"Hey, Alan, did you have any issues from anything we ate recently? My stomach has been hurting, and now the pain is awful."

"I haven't had any problems," my husband replied. "Do you have any other symptoms?"

"No fever, but something feels strange. I think I need to go to the doctor." This was a pain that I had never experienced.

I was able to get an appointment the same day. I arrived at the office early, checked in at the front desk, and found a seat in the waiting room. The pain began to come in waves. One minute I was comfortable and the next minute, I was sweating, grimacing, and hugging my abdomen with a tight grip.

After a short time, a nurse opened the door to the patient rooms and called my name. She did a preliminary check-in, and then I was alone until the doctor came in.

The pain had ceased before she entered the room. As we chatted about my condition, a sudden sharp pain caused me to lean forward and cry out.

"Are you having an attack right now?"

"Yes, this is awful. What's happening to me?" Teardrops raced down my face.

"I'm not sure. Let's do some bloodwork and an X-ray of your abdomen. Then we'll know how to proceed with a plan of treatment."

I had wanted a quick fix, but the doctor wanted to rule out certain conditions. I left the office and went immediately to the outpatient area to have the tests completed.

Waves of pain left and returned while I waited. Sounds from the television playing in the background were no distraction.

A short time passed, and my name was called. Blood was drawn, and I was told that the results would be sent to my doctor. But as my X-ray was completed, the technician asked, "Mrs. Henderson, I know you're here for stomach issues, but did anyone tell you there is a spot on your lung?"

"No." My anxiety skyrocketed. "A spot on my lung?" The scan was supposed to be for my abdomen.

"Yes. This scan included your lungs, too. We'll get this report to your doctor immediately."

I returned home. Evening came and the pain increased again. I couldn't find a comfortable position to sleep in. I woke Alan and shared my concern. "We need to go to the emergency room. The pain is worse."

Arriving at the hospital, I followed the same routine as earlier in the day for check-in. The waiting room was empty, which was odd for that time of night. My name was called almost as soon as we sat in the patient intake area.

A review of the symptoms and another scan were performed. Then, the same question. "Have you been told there is a spot on your right lung?"

Two times in one day I had been alerted to a suspicious area on my lung.

I explained about the earlier visit to my doctor. After my chart was reviewed, I was given pain medicine and a muscle relaxer, and we returned home.

The next day, my doctor called to schedule testing with a specific focus on my lungs. After those results continued to show a suspicious area, I was given the option of meeting with a pulmonologist.

The pulmonologist agreed that my lungs needed to be monitored. Additional scans in the months that followed showed the spot had not grown, but now that we are aware of it, we can continue to monitor the area and make sure everything continues to be OK. As an eighteen-year breast cancer survivor, any suspicious spot can be cause for concern.

I thank God for that abdominal pain that was severe enough to send me to the doctor and hospital. Without the issue in my stomach, the spot on my lung may not have been found.

My stomach pain left and has not returned. The cause was never determined.

Thank You, God, for my stomach pain.

God's Mysterious Ways: The Why

Why does a person have a mysterious pain that sends them to the doctor—and then promptly disappears? Or a sudden impulse to linger when they're already running late?

Sometimes the "why" of a situation becomes obvious very quickly, as it did for the authors in many stories throughout this volume. But sometimes it never becomes obvious. How do we make sense of events in our lives, especially painful ones, that don't seem to have an explanation?

What if the really important question isn't why, but Who? Who can we turn to when we need strength or support? Who is with us no matter what happens, no matter what we do? When we keep the answer to that question in mind, everything else comes into focus.

- **Pray.** When you're tempted to pray *why*, instead try praying just for God to be there: to be a loving presence and a guiding light in the lives of whoever needs Him.

- **Seek.** Have you been in a situation, or witnessed a situation, where you didn't understand the whys of what was happening? What happens if you shift your perspective to Who?

- **Act.** In moments of confusion, take a step back, remember the gift of trust, and give everything to Him.

- **Reflect.** How often do you find that God is not only the Who, but the Why as well?

Golden Chariots Don't Run on Fumes

Sarah Greek

*I will turn all my mountains into roads,
and my highways will be raised up.*

—Isaiah 49:11 (NIV)

For a young couple, obtaining a used car without going into debt was agonizing. Salesmen tried to hustle us into "deals" we couldn't afford, and too-good-to-be-true prices often hid expensive problems like rusting undercarriages or transmission issues. While test driving one promising car, it actually broke down and we were stranded! We tried our best to laugh through it even as we hiked back to the dealership. "Who else has this kind of luck?" we asked ourselves.

Not having a car was making our commutes to work increasingly stressful, but we really didn't want to purchase outside our means. We followed up on lead after lead and ran into scam after scam—or worse still, radio silence from sellers we reached out to from ads. I could hardly believe how many people were trying to sell cars but just couldn't be bothered to answer their phone!

One day, I found yet another "amazing" deal on a classified page—low price, low mileage, family-sized car. *This one can't possibly be real, either,* I thought to myself, and I sent an inquiry without hope of a response. The car looked practically new. There was no way that the listed price was correct, unless there was something majorly wrong with the car or it was just another fake ad.

I did receive a response, though. The person on the other end of the call was personable and genuine, explaining that the car had belonged to their aging parents, who kept it parked in a garage and drove it only for short trips to the supermarket and back—hence the low mileage. They were trying to clear out their parents' belongings and settle their estate and just wanted things gone fast, hence the low price. We joked about that being exactly what someone would say if they were trying to pull a scam, but the more we talked, the more comfortable I felt that this was the real deal.

The only tricky, sticky bit was their location, which was a bit far away. At the time we were relying on friends for rides, and it was a little too much to ask of them. We struggled to figure out how we would get to them to see the car and make the deal before someone else snapped it up! We asked them if they would hold it for us, explaining our distance issue and not having a car. Their response was completely unexpected.

"Your name sounds familiar. Are you by chance the Sarah G. who directs the musicals at the Bible Baptist School in Mechanicsburg?" I was in fact the one and same. "Our grandson is involved in the musical this year for the first time. The whole family has been just amazed at the change in his confidence and exuberance. He speaks highly of you and how much fun you make the rehearsals and the whole experience. We are really very grateful for all you do with the kids there and the impact it is making. We will absolutely hold the car for you. And, as we will be coming to see our grandson in the show, we can bring the car there and make it easier for you to make the transaction."

Once again we thought to ourselves, "Who has this kind of luck?" After so much time looking, so many cars, and so many frustrating encounters, what are the odds that we would find the perfect car from a seller who already knew me? We shook our heads in amazement and agreed: Christ trumps Craigslist every time!

A Prayer Quickly Answered

Barbara Jean Deaton

For the eyes of the Lord are on the righteous and his ears are attentive to their prayer...
—1 Peter 3:12 (NIV)

I was taking a masters-level research class at a university in order to be qualified to teach English at a Bible college. I knew before I took this class that it would be a challenge, but I also thought it would better prepare me for guiding students through the process of creating their own research papers. In the years before online sources became the go-to for any type of research, homework consisted of spending hours in the library poring through reference materials, answering questions about obscure information and the sources where I found it. Although the work was time-consuming, I was enjoying the class and doing well.

Then came the midterm exam. The test was a practical exercise, like the homework that had come before it, that required searching for answers in specified locations throughout the library and the limited online resources that existed at the time. Each student's midterm was different, so we could not depend on each other for help.

I began searching in the library reference section days before the exam was due, because I wanted to have plenty of time to find the correct answers. The format of the test gave me time to search and think. I made notes on where I thought the answers were, so that I could go back to retrieve the requested information once I was sure that I had found the right book, magazine, or online source.

The days flew by, and the paper was due soon. Once again I was at the university library working on the midterm. But after reviewing the information I'd gathered already, I realized that I wasn't sure I had the right answers for many of the questions. When the test said "provide the source judged to be the fullest discussion of drama in English modernism," had I found *the* correct discussion, or was there a better one out there? When asked to "provide a study which explains the connection between modernism and revolution in style," had I found the right study, or did the teacher want a different one?

I wanted to make a good grade on this midterm. Over half of the questions were either not finished, or I was not sure the answers I had were correct. I held up the midterm and prayed. "Lord, you see all the things on this test that I do not have completed, and you see all the things on this test that I am not sure are done correctly. Please help me to find them. Amen."

Returning to the reference section where I knew one of the answers should be, I began searching through one of the books again. When I looked up, I saw my professor coming toward me. I couldn't believe it! I had never seen her in the library on that day of the week, since it was not the day we had class.

As we greeted each other, she asked me how I was doing. I told her I was having trouble finding the answers because I wanted to make sure I got the correct ones, and I was sure that one was in that reference section. I asked her about some of the questions on the test. She helped me to fully understand what I needed to know and gave me assurance that I was searching for the answers in the right places. Then she explained to me that she only helped me because she saw that I was already on the right track.

After my teacher left, I just stood there praising and thanking God for answering that prayer so quickly and in such an amazing way! No sooner had I prayed for help than He sent my teacher walking toward me.

When I looked up, I saw my professor coming toward me. I couldn't believe it! I had never seen her in the library on that day of the week.

I finished that test with a rejoicing heart. God showed me He cares! He does help His children when we face difficult situations in life. He used my teacher to help me, and later, in the spirit of allowing God to use me, I was able to help another student who was struggling.

With God's help, I earned an excellent grade in that class, and went on to become qualified to teach English at my favorite Bible college. I still use those research skills to help my own students become better writers. And it never would have happened if God hadn't heard my prayer and sent my teacher to me at exactly the right time.

The Only Night We Needed Help

Jesse Neve

And we know that for those who love God all things work together for good, for those who are called according to his purpose.

—Romans 8:28 (ESV)

Six hundred and seventy-six car rides spanning thirteen years. Around three thousand hours in the car. Our guardian angel was with my father and me on every trip, but one night, that angel sent an additional special helper.

My parents divorced when I was five. A year later, my mom and stepdad and I relocated to a town two hours from my dad's house. Their agreement was that I would spend every other weekend with Papa. And I did, without fail, until I graduated from high school. During all of that time, *one* Minnesota snowstorm made Papa a couple of hours late. Aside from that, there was only one other time we ran into problems, which is miraculous within itself.

Papa and I loved our drives together. Every other Friday, he would get off of work and drive straight to pick me up. I knew he would arrive at 6:15 and I was usually outside waiting in anticipation for him, perched atop our wooden fence. I would see his little brown Ford turning down the long driveway, and I would take off running across the yard to meet him.

After we loaded my mound of luggage into his car, we would drive away and he would say, "Tell me about your day."

I always began with, "My alarm went off at 6:14 and . . ." I would walk my way through every class, everything we learned in each class, things my friends said or did, and what I ate for lunch. I told him every detail up until, "and then you pulled in the driveway." It was a wonderful tradition that was not only fun for me, but he greatly enjoyed hearing about my everyday life since he didn't see me on a daily basis. I talked pretty much the entire two hours of our Friday night drives. And I can still clearly picture the side of Papa's face as he was driving, smiling and asking questions about my news. He was completely focused on the pictures I was painting as we drove down the road.

In all of those years, until my high school years, when I occasionally brought a friend with me for the weekend, we never had a single other person ride along when Papa came to pick me up—except once. That one evening, when I was about eight, I ran to meet Papa's car in our driveway and I was surprised to see that there was someone in the passenger seat. I recognized her as Papa's friend Donna from work. I found out later that she was going through some hard times and needed someone to talk to. Papa had offered to let her ride along so they could have the two hours to chat.

That night, everything was going along smoothly. We were about halfway back to Papa's house when Papa quickly pulled the car to the side of the road. "Get out," he said sternly. "Donna, take Jesse down into the ditch, away from the car."

We both did as we were told, not knowing what was happening. Papa disappeared around the back of the car and then we waited. I was scared. Here I was standing in a dark ditch with a lady I hardly knew, cars whizzing by at high speed, uncertainty eating at me. Were we in danger? Was Papa? Donna put her arm around me protectively as we stood in silence, neither of us knowing what would happen next. I was thankful that she was there with me, thankful to not be in the ditch alone.

The minutes dragged on. Finally Papa appeared around the front of the car and called, "OK, it's fine. We can go now." We got back into the car and drove off.

As it turned out, our car had run over a brown paper bag. Papa didn't think anything of it, except that moments later, in the rearview mirror, he saw sparks coming out from behind the car. The bag had been snagged on the underside of the car and caught on fire. Papa was able to hook the flaming bag and remove it safely from the car before anything more serious happened.

At the time, I was just glad we could get on with our drive. We dropped Donna off at her car back at their workplace and resumed our normal weekend. It took me years to realize the significance of that night. The *only* night, in all of those years, that I needed someone there to protect me, to help hold back the fear in the dark ditch of a busy highway, Donna was there.

Thank you, guardian angel, for keeping us safe all of those years.

If Only Mother Were Here

Roberta Messner

As a mother comforts her child, so I will comfort you.
—Isaiah 66:13 (NIV)

After a devastating fall and months of relentless rehab, I was finally coming home. In the ambulance en route to my beloved log cabin that December morning, I tried to imagine what it would be like, what my old place would even look like. It had been so long. To even dream of being at home and resuming my old life seemed a recipe for disappointment.

Strapped to the gurney, I felt the gravel crunch of wheels touching my driveway as the driver turned in. The sweet, efficient lady who'd attended me dashed inside to check things out. From the corner of my ear I heard the voice of my sister, Rebekkah. Because of the COVID quarantine I hadn't seen her in weeks, but she'd been busy, busy, busy taking on the role of my caregiver, a job with no guaranteed finish line. Converting my cabin into a makeshift hospital.

I was beyond grateful for my sister and friends who'd pitched in to help. Still, I longed for my mother. Back in 1973, she'd suffered her own terrible fall with a brain bleed. She recovered, but she was not quite the mother I remembered after that. It was my own greatest fear, the possibility of not ever being the same Roberta. Mother had battled through a long road to recovery to regain her ability to serve her church, her neighborhood, and her community. She alone could tell me how to do that. How to live again when an accident had taken so much. My mother, who'd found more ways to love people than anyone I'd ever known—yet had never totally regained that quality after her accident, though other compensatory ones gave her a better-than-ever loveliness.

Mother's extravagant caregiving was a quality the two of us shared. As a child I'd been diagnosed with an incurable condition that caused tumors to grow throughout my body. She'd given up her teaching position to assure me the best life possible. Ever my advocate, she began a search for state-of-the-art treatments that found us on Greyhound buses and trains and in endless doctors' waiting rooms. She came alive in those places, was a magnet for troubled, hurting people. Her canvas tote brimmed with books, homemade blackberry preserves, clippings from magazines, and anything else that might lift a spirit.

On the pediatrics ward she scurried from room to room, gathering up laundry from parents who'd stayed the night or doling out treasures. The real treasure was Mother. During my last hospitalization before her fall, I'd had a roommate she particularly adored. Keren, spelled with Es. Keren who, like me, had a brain tumor, and was trying to learn to talk and walk again. Like me, Keren had missed a lot of school. The teacher in Mother kicked in.

Keren had been distraught the morning they took me for the craniotomy. After they transferred me to the gurney, Mother kissed my forehead, then went to Keren's bedside. I watched as her teaching instinct took over. "You don't have to say the big words, honey. Try *walk. Love. Can.*" On the way to another cold operating room, Mother's words to my roommate warmed me. Keren would make it—I would make it—because my mother knew the best words of all.

One cold January night, not too long after I'd come home, the fireplace warmed my cabin. Not my spirit. It was nearly three a.m. With my sister sound asleep upstairs, the blackness closed in on me. *If only Mother were here*, I agonized. *If she were here, she'd know just what to say, convince me I could get out of this bed, be independent again.* What was the use in even thinking such a thing? To dream of her nurturing presence, the promise of her words? My hospital bed was in the very spot where Mother's had been when I cared for her those last weeks. Where twenty-three years before she'd left this world for heaven. Left me.

When I could stand it no more, I reached for my cell phone. I'd just gotten a replacement. It had so many unfamiliar options and buttons I could barely dial a number. Wondering what I could look at that might bring a smidgen of comfort, I had an odd thought. There was this writer I adored who told stories about the small town where he grew up. He had the most charming grandma who reminded me of Mother. Even his pen name, Viola Shipman, honored her.

With my paltry Internet skills and new phone, it was a stretch to think that I could find him. If I could type her name, maybe—just maybe—an interview of him talking about her would pop up. I could pretend he was talking about Mother, make it through this impossibly lonely night. I tapped in Viola Shipman and waited. When nothing happened, I hit every button on that phone. *Viola. Viola. Mother. Mother.*

Somebody out there! Help me!

Mother's extravagant caregiving was a quality the two of us shared.

At long last, the author of the Viola Shipman books appeared. Then, just as quickly, vanished. In his place was the Guideposts Facebook page. This was even stranger than my idea to type in "Viola." I wasn't on Facebook, never looked at it, didn't have any kind of shortcuts on my phone that would have brought it up, let alone taken me specifically to this page. Yet here it was.

In the post that had appeared on my screen, readers were talking about something I'd written seven years before. *Guideposts* Editor-in Chief Edward Grinnan had added a comment. Suddenly, the posts I had been looking at were replaced by an entry from a reader by the name of Keren Fitzgerald. A chill ran up and down my spine. It couldn't be. Not Keren, my hospital roommate from 1972. My last surgery before my caregiver-mother's fall.

I couldn't breathe. In the half century since, I'd never met anyone with that particular spelling of Keren.

I haven't read Guideposts *for years and only then it was that I came across a copy in a doctor's office. I met you, Roberta, in Timken Mercy Hospital in 1972. I was nine years old. You were so kind and loving, and your mother, too. I remember when she came to visit you. I thought she was coming to visit me.*

Across the whispers of time, the babbling-brook voice that soothed my heart strings returned to me. My mother's! Keren continued:

What love she gave to me I cannot fathom. I know that her sweet attitude rubbed off on my mother. God sent her to show my mom what a precious thing it is to have a daughter. Not all moms are equipped, or want to be, for raising children. My life was better after having been in the same hospital room with you.

Mother's words were as alive as they'd been a half century before. It was as if I'd suddenly been blessed with what I'd been yearning for, the presence of my mother—the consummate comforting one before her fall. The one who was there to catch me when *I* fell.

She was there with me, in my heart, my secret self. I would fight for recovery, just as she had. And she would be there to catch me if I fell.

Three months later, I was milling around the grounds of my cabin when the wheels of a red, white, and blue van crunched the gravel driveway. As the driver closed his door, he pointed to the name of his company, then smiled in my direction. "Now this is what I call *Active Medical*," he said with a chuckle. "We don't usually find the patient in the yard."

If only Mother were here. If she were here, she'd know just what to say, convince me I could get out of this bed, be independent again.

I watched as he hoisted my wheelchair, walker, and hospital bed through the doorway, then loaded it all up. I wouldn't need them anymore. In one instant I went from a bedbound patient to—I wasn't sure what.

I ventured back inside to the glaringly empty room. It was just as it had been when Mother died and they came for everything. For a moment I felt barren as well. But only for a moment. My mother was no longer lost to me. From her home in heaven she spoke no words, yet I heard every one of them. *LIVE, Roberta. LOVE. WALK into your future.*

My new eyes took in my living room. It was exactly that, a place for living. I walked into my new life, full to overflowing with my mother's love.

241

Acknowledgments

Every attempt has been made to credit the sources of copyrighted material used in this book. If any such acknowledgment has been inadvertently omitted or miscredited, receipt of such information would be appreciated.

Scripture quotations marked (CSB) are taken from *The Christian Standard Bible*, copyright © 2017 by Holman Bible Publishers. Used by permission.

Scripture quotations marked (ESV) are taken from *The Holy Bible, English Standard Version*. Copyright © 2001 by Crossway Bibles, a division of Good News Publishers. Used by permission. All rights reserved.

Scripture quotations marked (JPS) are taken from *Tanakh: A New Translation of the Holy Scriptures according to the Traditional Hebrew Text*. Copyright © 1985 by the Jewish Publication Society. All rights reserved.

Scripture quotations marked (KJV) are taken from the *King James Version of the Bible*.

Scripture quotations marked (MSG) are taken from *The Message*. Copyright © 1993, 2002, 2018 by Eugene H. Peterson.

Scripture quotations marked (NASB) are taken from the *New American Standard Bible*®, Copyright © 1960, 1971, 1977, 1995, 2020 by The Lockman Foundation. All rights reserved.

Scripture quotations marked (NIV) are taken from *The Holy Bible, New International Version*®, *NIV*®. Copyright © 1973, 1978, 1984, 2011 by Biblica, Inc. Used by permission. All rights reserved worldwide.

Scripture quotations marked (NKJV) are taken from the *New King James Version*®. Copyright © 1982 by Thomas Nelson. Used by permission. All rights reserved.

Scripture quotations marked (NLT) are taken from the *Holy Bible, New Living Translation*. Copyright © 1996, 2004, 2007, 2015 by Tyndale House Foundation. Used by permission of Tyndale House Publishers Inc., Carol Stream, Illinois. All rights reserved.

Scripture quotations marked (NRSVUE) are taken from the *New Revised Standard Version, Updated Edition*. Copyright © 2021 National Council of Churches of Christ in the United States of America. Used by permission. All rights reserved worldwide.

A Note from the Editors

We hope you enjoyed *Heavenly Interventions*, published by Guideposts. For more than seventy-five years, Guideposts, a nonprofit organization, has been driven by a vision of a world filled with hope. We aspire to be the voice of a trusted friend, a friend who makes you feel more hopeful and connected.

By making a purchase from Guideposts, you join our community in touching millions of lives, inspiring them to believe that all things are possible through faith, hope, and prayer. Your continued support allows us to provide uplifting resources to those in need. Whether through our communities, websites, apps, or publications, we inspire our audiences, bring them together, and comfort, uplift, entertain, and guide them. Visit us at guideposts.org to learn more.

We would love to hear from you. Write us at Guideposts, P.O. Box 5815, Harlan, Iowa 51593 or call us at (800) 932-2145. Did you love *Heavenly Interventions?* Leave a review for this product on guideposts.org/shop. Your feedback helps others in our community find relevant products.

Find inspiration, find faith, find Guideposts.

Shop our best sellers and favorites at
guideposts.org/shop
Or scan the QR code to go directly to our Shop